WITHDRAWN

J. S. Bach's
Great Eighteen Organ Chorales

J. S. BACH'S

Great Eighteen Organ Chorales

Russell Stinson

OXFORD

UNIVERSITY PRESS

2001

OXFORD
UNIVERSITY PRESS

Oxford   New York
Athens   Auckland   Bangkok   Bogotá   Buenos Aires   Calcutta
Cape Town   Chennai   Dar es Salaam   Delhi   Florence   Hong Kong   Istanbul
Karachi   Kuala Lumpur   Madrid   Melbourne   Mexico City   Mumbai
Nairobi   Paris   São Paulo   Shanghai   Singapore   Taipei   Tokyo   Toronto   Warsaw

and associated companies in
Berlin   Ibadan

Copyright © 2001 by Oxford University Press

Published by Oxford University Press, Inc.
198 Madison Avenue, New York, New York 10016

Oxford is a registered trademark of Oxford University Press.

Library of Congress Cataloging-in-Publication Data
Stinson, Russell.
J. S. Bach's great eighteen organ chorales / Russell Stinson.
p.   cm.
Includes bibliographical references.
ISBN 0-19-511666-6
1. Bach, Johann Sebastian, 1685–1750. Choräle von verschiedener Art,
BWV 651–668. 2. Chorale prelude.   I. Title: Great eighteen organ chorales.   II. Title:
J. S. Bach's great 18 organ chorales.   III. Title: Great 18 organ chorales: IV. Title.
ML410.B13 S89   2000
786.5′189925′092—dc21   00-023687

1 3 5 7 9 8 6 4 2

Printed in the United States of America
on acid-free paper

To Laurie,
on her fortieth birthday

PREFACE

The "Great Eighteen" chorales (BWV 651–68) are undeniably among Bach's most celebrated works for the organ. The collection has long been championed by organists as church and concert repertory and recognized by scholars as a milestone in the history of the organ chorale. Not surprisingly, the music has also spawned a vast literature.

Still, most of these writings either superficially cover the entire set or dwell on single pieces. In this monograph I hope to satisfy the need for a comprehensive study of the Great Eighteen, one that discusses the individual settings in detail *and* places the collection as a whole in a broader context. I also attempt to bring the English-speaking reader up-to-date on such critical matters as the chronology and stylistic orientation of the music, while allowing ample room for my own observations. This book is the first in any language devoted to these masterpieces.

In the opening chapter ("Compositional Models and Musical Style"), I consider the stylistic background of the music, with an eye to its stunning originality. Admittedly, in certain pieces Bach closely imitated the chorale types of his predecessors. But for the most part he chose boldly to combine these types with such "secular" genres as the concerto and trio sonata. The Great Eighteen therefore illustrate two general patterns: the elevation of preexisting forms to their highest possible level and the invention of various hybrid designs.

The second chapter ("The Genesis of the Collection") takes a close look at the autograph manuscript. It seeks to draw the reader into the

always fascinating world of Bach's workshop and to eavesdrop on the
master as, piece by piece, he compiles this source. Central to the discussion here is the issue of compositional process, for the manuscript—contrary to what scholars have previously implied—preserves
many compositional emendations. We will also investigate how Bach's
entries in this source compare musically to the preliminary versions of
the chorales found elsewhere.

Chapter 3 ("Significance") examines the different "identities" of the
Great Eighteen, as well as the structure of the collection. Since Bach
composed the works for worship services in his capacity as a church
organist, their original purpose may have been rather pragmatic.
Decades later, though, when he decided to revise the pieces and assemble them into the present set, the intent behind the music had obviously changed. For one thing, Bach's position at that time did not re-
quire him to produce organ music of any kind.

Chapter 4 ("The Music and Its Performance") offers commentaries
on the individual settings. Here various aspects of the music come into
play, including contrapuntal and harmonic structure and textual-musi-
cal relationships. The Great Eighteen also pose intriguing problems of
performance practice: registration, ornamentation, and tempo, to name
but a few. It is to be hoped that even the most experienced organist will
find in this chapter new ways not only of thinking about these pieces
but also of playing them.

The fifth and final chapter ("Reception History") traces the various
roles played by the Great Eighteen in Western music from Bach's lifetime to the present. Happily, the dramatis personae of this story include
many of the greatest composers in music history: Johannes Brahms,
César Franck, Felix Mendelssohn, Max Reger, Arnold Schoenberg,
Robert Schumann, and Ralph Vaughan Williams.

This book could not have been written without the help of a great
many institutions and individuals. I would like to thank, first of all, Dr.
Helmut Hell and the staff of the Staatsbibliothek zu Berlin for allowing
me to examine firsthand Bach's autograph manuscript of the Great
Eighteen. Thanks are also due to the Staatsbibliothek zu Berlin, Bach-
Archiv Leipzig, Leipziger Städtische Bibliotheken, Johann-Sebastian-
Bach-Institut (Göttingen), Kunstsammlungen zu Weimar, and Univer-
sity of Pennsylvania Libraries for providing me with photocopies of
sources in their possession. I am grateful to Lawrence Archbold, David
Buice, Dean Covington, Reinmar Emans, Marjorie Hassen, Karen
Holyer, Robin Leaver, Teryn McDuff, William Peterson, and Peter
Wollny for assistance of various kinds and to Kathy Whittenton for her
help in tracking down secondary sources. A special word of apprecia-

tion goes to Kevin Jackson, who for two years was my research assistant on this project. For supporting my work in the form of travel grants I would like to thank the administration of Lyon College. My deepest debt is to Maribeth Payne of Oxford University Press for her cooperation and patience during all stages of this enterprise and for suggesting a book on the Great Eighteen in the first place.

Batesville, Arkansas   R. S.
December 1999

CONTENTS

ABBREVIATIONS

BuxWV   *Buxtehude-Werke-Verzeichnis.* Georg Karstädt, *Thematisch-systematisches Verzeichnis der musikalischen Werke von Dietrich Buxtehude* (Wiesbaden: Breitkopf & Härtel, 1974).

BWV   *Bach-Werke-Verzeichnis.* Wolfgang Schmieder, *Thematisch-systematisches Verzeichnis der musikalischen Werke Johann Sebastian Bachs* (Leipzig: Breitkopf & Härtel, 1950; revised edition, Wiesbaden: Breitkopf & Härtel, 1990).

KB   *Kritischer Bericht* (critical report of the *Neue Bach-Ausgabe*).

NBA   *Neue Bach-Ausgabe. Johann Sebastian Bach: Neue Ausgabe sämtlicher Werke* (Kassel: Bärenreiter; Leipzig: VEB Deutscher Verlag für Musik, 1954–present).

P   *Partitur* (music score; abbreviation used by the Staatsbibliothek zu Berlin—Preussischer Kulturbesitz, Musikabteilung mit Mendelssohn-Archiv).

SBB   Staatsbibliothek zu Berlin—Preussischer Kulturbesitz, Musikabteilung mit Mendelssohn-Archiv.

J. S. Bach's
Great Eighteen Organ Chorales

Chapter 1

COMPOSITIONAL MODELS
AND MUSICAL STYLE

❧

With the possible exception of the *Well-Tempered Clavier*, the Great Eighteen chorales are the most diverse collection of pieces Bach ever wrote. Extremely innovative works coexist with rather conservative ones; densely textured settings for full organ stand alongside delicate trios. As Peter Williams has suggested, variety of idiom may have been a "guiding principle" of the set.[1]

One way of understanding this diversity is through the preexisting forms taken by Bach as compositional models. While some of these come directly from the organ music of his predecessors, others are borrowed from such disparate realms as orchestral, chamber, and even dance music. We will take into account the models themselves, their use by Bach in general, and their appropriation within these eighteen pieces.

First, some definitions. "Organ chorale" will refer to any organ work based on a chorale tune. (Although "chorale prelude" is often used to mean the same thing, this formulation is best reserved for pieces specifically written to introduce congregational hymns.) What is meant by "chorale" is a congregational hymn of the Lutheran church. Strophic in design and sung in the vernacular, this creation of Martin Luther has been called the very soul of his denomination. It took several decades beyond the Reformation itself, but by the late sixteenth century organists routinely performed on chorale melodies during worship.[2] These performances often took the form of improvisations, but notated arrangements were not uncommon. By 1685, the year of Bach's birth, literally thousands of organ chorales had been committed to paper.

As a young man, Bach contributed mightily to this tradition. Of his roughly two hundred extant organ chorales, as many as fifty probably originated before 1707, the year he became organist at the Church of St. Blasius in Mühlhausen. These juvenilia demonstrate well the budding composer's fluency with all the organ-chorale types of the day.

On the basis of their relatively sophisticated style, none of the Great Eighteen could have been composed before this date. Except possibly for the final work in the set, "Vor deinen Thron tret ich hiermit," they all exist in early versions whose sources date from Bach's tenure as court organist in Weimar, which lasted from 1708 to 1717. Thus, none of them could have been composed after 1717.

In all but one instance, these sources are not autographs but manuscript copies penned by two members of Bach's Weimar circle: Johann Gottfried Walther, a cousin of Bach and organist at the town church of Weimar while Bach was there; and Johann Tobias Krebs, who first studied under Walther from about 1710 to 1714 and then under Bach from about 1714 to 1717.[3] Unfortunately, it is not possible to assign any of these sources to specific years within Bach's Weimar period. Rather, in dating these early versions one must rely heavily on issues of musical style.

THE CHORALE MOTET

Conceived along the lines of the Renaissance vocal motet, the chorale motet emerged at the turn of the seventeenth century and quickly became a favorite form of the central-German organ school. Its modus operandi is merely to establish each phrase of the chorale as a point of imitation, always using the same basic rhythms for each imitative statement (as opposed to a concluding statement in augmentation). Depending on the length of the tune, the technique can become monotonous, which might explain why Bach left behind only a few youthful specimens of this chorale type, including two ("Ehre sei dir, Christe, der du leidest Not" and "Nun lasst uns den Leib begraben") from the recently discovered Neumeister Collection of organ chorales from the Bach circle. Perhaps as he matured as a composer, Bach found the severity of the chorale motet a hindrance to his creativity.

The Great Eighteen contain three chorale motets: the two settings of "Jesus Christus, unser Heiland," the first with pedal, the second for manuals alone; and the second arrangement of "Komm, Heiliger Geist, Herre Gott." They are likely among the first pieces in the collection to have been composed, and for reasons other than just the presence of this chorale type. For, as Jean-Claude Zehnder has recently shown, all three settings are very similar in style to church cantatas composed by Bach during his year in Mühlhausen (1707–8).[4] Accordingly, Zehnder dates these three organ chorales to this year as well.

In an impressive series of articles on Bach's early style, Zehnder has brought such evidence to bear on many of the Great Eighteen chorales.[5] His findings have greatly clarified how these works relate to the music of Bach's predecessors and contemporaries and how they compare to other compositions—particularly church cantatas—by Bach himself. At the same time, Zehnder has proposed a convincing, albeit tentative, chronology of the individual pieces according to their early versions (whose BWV numbers normally include the suffix "a"). His research forms the basis of the present chapter.

Returning to Bach's Mühlhausen cantatas, which are the composer's earliest, one of their hallmarks is the depiction of individual lines and even individual words of the text. Whereas this procedure achieves a particularly close correspondence between text and music, in agreement with Luther's notion of "the proclamation of the word,"[6] Bach often applies it with sufficient emphasis to fragment a single movement into several distinct sections. Two of the chorale motets from the Great Eighteen use similar techniques. The *pedaliter* "Jesus Christus, unser Heiland" changes countermelodies between phrases for the sake of text painting, while the "Komm, Heiliger Geist" arrangement ends with a veritable flurry of notes to symbolize the word "Hallelujah." That the bass voice of the *pedaliter* "Jesus Christus" vacillates between manual and pedal is a further sign of an early date.[7]

The last movement of the most famous of the Mühlhausen cantatas, *Gottes Zeit ist die allerbeste Zeit*, BWV 106, and the *manualiter* "Jesus Christus, unser Heiland" offer a further analogy. Both are chorale settings whose basic rhythm changes midway through from quarters and eighths, respectively, to sixteenth notes. In neither instance, though, does this unusual acceleration seem textually motivated.

Bach's organ chorale "Valet will ich dir geben," BWV 735a, whose earliest source dates from circa 1708–10, provides additional evidence that the three chorale motets from the Great Eighteen are relatively early. As Zehnder points out, not only is this work also a chorale motet, but much of its figuration is virtually identical to that of the *pedaliter* "Jesus Christus, unser Heiland." In both pieces, the chorale tune tends to sound against the same two motives—a dotted rhythm and a disjunct, syncopated figure—which are integrated to produce continuous motion in sixteenth notes (see Examples 1-1 and 1-2). Bach's model here with respect to form and figuration was probably Georg Böhm, or-

EXAMPLE 1-1. "Valet will ich dir geben," BWV 735a

EXAMPLE 1-2. "Jesus Christus, unser Heiland," BWV 665a

ganist at St. John's Church in Lüneburg while Bach was a student there from 1700 to 1702 and an important composer of chorale motets.[8]

THE CHORALE PARTITA

The chorale partita is simply a set of variations on a chorale melody. Typically, each variation presents the complete tune, and the variations function as independent movements. The earliest surviving examples, which imitate the variation style of the English virginalists, are by the Dutch master Jan Pieterszoon Sweelinck (1562–1621). Sweelinck, in turn, passed on the design to his German pupils Samuel Scheidt and

Heinrich Scheidemann. By the turn of the eighteenth century, the chorale partita was closely associated with central Germany, most notably with the Thuringians Georg Böhm (who grew up in Thuringia but worked in northern Germany) and Johann Pachelbel. Böhm, in particular, was a profound influence on Bach's earliest works of this type.

Bach's chorale partitas range from youthful *manualiter* settings such as "O Gott, du frommer Gott" to the very late Canonic Variations on "Vom Himmel hoch." The two Great Eighteen chorales that qualify, "Komm, Gott Schöpfer, Heiliger Geist" and "O Lamm Gottes, unschuldig," pose notable exceptions to the norm. They contain only two and three variations, respectively, and in each work the music flows without any pause from one variation to the next. In the case of "O Lamm Gottes," Bach's use of three variations corresponds to the number of stanzas in the chorale text. His use of only two variations for "Komm, Gott Schöpfer" has no obvious rationale.

Chorale partitas such as these that dispense with the customary breaks between variations are exceedingly rare. Indeed, perhaps the only other examples are Dietrich Buxtehude's "Nun lob, mein Seel, den Herren," BuxWV 213, and Johann Michael Bach's "Meine Seele erhebt den Herren."[9] Like "O Lamm Gottes," both of these works contain only three variations, although the chorales themselves have five and eleven stanzas, respectively. As in both of J. S. Bach's partitas, the last variation of Buxtehude's presents the chorale tune in the pedals.

Buxtehude's huge impact on the young J. S. Bach has long been acknowledged, and we will discuss this topic in more detail vis-à-vis the ornamental chorale. As for J. M. Bach (1648–94), the father of Johann Sebastian's first wife, the unearthing of the Neumeister Collection has shown that he, too, was an important model for the young Sebastian Bach, especially in terms of musical form, texture, and harmonic vocabulary.[10] It is quite possible, then, that one or both of these partitas served as prototypes for "O Lamm Gottes" and perhaps "Komm, Gott Schöpfer" as well.

"O Lamm Gottes" may also be one of the earliest of the Great Eighteen chorales, for the way in which Bach depicts the word *verzagen* ("despair") in the third variation agrees completely with his Mühlhausen cantata style. Exactly at this point in the piece, descending chromatic lines suddenly appear, and the meter switches from compound to simple triple. Bach uses precisely this type of chromaticism to symbolize grief in the second movement of the Mühlhausen cantata *Gott ist mein König*, BWV 71, and in the *pedaliter* "Jesus Christus, unser Heiland" from the Great Eighteen. Because of its relationship to the Mühlhausen cantatas, Zehnder assigns "O Lamm Gottes" to 1707–8.

"Komm, Gott Schöpfer" is clearly later. Its first variation, according to the early version, is a carbon copy of a work (BWV 631a) from Bach's *Orgelbüchlein* that was composed directly into the autograph of that collection between 1709 and 1713.[11] Therefore, this Great Eighteen chorale must have originated sometime between 1709 and 1717, when Bach left Weimar.

THE ORNAMENTAL CHORALE

The idea behind the ornamental chorale is to present the complete hymn melody in one voice, usually the soprano, amid profuse embellishment. Evidently the brainchild of Sweelinck's pupil Heinrich Scheidemann, this chorale type enjoyed great popularity in northern Germany. Its greatest and most prolific advocate was Dietrich Buxtehude, whose thirty-odd specimens are notable for their use of expressive, "vocal" embellishments.

Virtually all these early ornamental settings indicate that the embellished chorale tune is to be played alone on the *Rückpositiv*, a manual division located behind the player and a standard feature on north-German instruments of the time. In most churches, the *Rückpositiv* was also the division of the organ closest to the congregation, which is why composers considered it so appropriate for this purpose. In central Germany, the *Positiv* division was represented by an *Oberwerk* or *Brustpositiv* situated in the main case. Still, an organist could easily achieve a timbral contrast between keyboard divisions by means of contrasting stops.

According to our definition, no fewer than seven of the Great Eighteen chorales qualify as ornamental chorales, making this the most common chorale type in the whole collection. (Two of these works are trios, and we will discuss them later in connection with that chorale type.) In each instance, Bach gives the embellished hymn melody its own manual. One sees soon enough, though, that far more is involved here than a bow to tradition. Rather, in these seven masterpieces Bach thoroughly transforms the ornamental chorale by granting unprecedented importance to the accompanimental voices (that is, the voices other than the one that states the chorale tune). By combining this chorale type with other compositional models he achieves a synthesis of incredible richness and intricacy.

Let us consider these works according to Zehnder's chronology, beginning with the second setting of "Komm, Heiliger Geist." If this title sounds familiar, it is because we have already categorized this piece as a chorale motet. Yet the presence of the ornamental chorale is indisputable: each point of imitation concludes with a lavishly decorated statement in the soprano, played on a separate manual.

Perhaps even more surprising than the conflation of these two chorale types is the evocation of French dance music, for this work also imitates the sarabande, the slow triple-meter dance commonly found in Baroque dance suites. Observe, for example, such classic traits of this dance type as the use of hemiola rhythms in the bass line to prepare for cadences and the regular accentuation of the second beat with a dotted quarter note.[12] The organ chorale is also sarabande-like in its use of stepwise melodic lines, French *agréments*, relatively slow rhythms, and, of course, triple meter. Such a model strongly suggests, once again, the influence of Georg Böhm, the most prolific composer of dance-based organ chorales before Bach. Bach was surely acquainted with the sarabande per se by his adolescence. According to his obituary, while a student in Lüneburg (1700–1702) he "acquired a thorough grounding in the French taste" from French musicians working in the nearby duchy of Celle.[13]

For reasons already discussed, Zehnder dates this setting of "Komm, Heiliger Geist" as 1707–8. Our next chorale appears to be somewhat later. It is the first of three arrangements in the Great Eighteen of "Allein Gott in der Höh sei Ehr" and Bach's most florid organ chorale of all. Whereas most of the ornamentation of the previous work was indicated by symbols (French practice), here it consists largely of runs in thirty-second and even sixty-fourth notes, much in the style of contemporary Italian violin music. These rhythms are extremely rare in Bach's Mühlhausen cantatas but quite standard in his earliest datable cantatas from Weimar, composed in 1713–14. One of these cantatas, *Ich hatte viel Bekümmernis*, BWV 21, offers an especially close parallel, since its introductory sinfonia—which makes regular use of these fast rhythms—includes in its penultimate bar a brief oboe cadenza. This setting of "Allein Gott" also concludes with a solo cadenza, a most unusual gesture for an organ chorale.

A further clue as to date of composition is how the accompanimental voices of this chorale refer throughout to the two themes stated at the outset by the inner parts (see Example 1-3). Such unanimity immediately brings to mind Bach's *Orgelbüchlein*, a collection of organ chorales distinguished by motivically unified accompaniments. Bach probably began work on the *Orgelbüchlein* early during his Weimar period, but by 1712 at the latest.[14] On the basis of this correspondence, plus those involving the cantatas, Zehnder dates this arrangement of "Allein Gott" as 1711–13.

The nature of this work's accompaniment also distances it from the ornamental chorales of the north-German organ school, particularly

EXAMPLE 1-3. "Allein Gott in der Höh sei Ehr," BWV 662a

those of Dietrich Buxtehude. While his settings do sometimes contain the sort of rapid ornamental figuration as described here, their accompanimental voices lack cohesion. He usually varies his accompaniment from phrase to phrase or writes chordal filler.

During the four months in 1705–6 that Bach studied in Lübeck under Buxtehude, the young composer might well have received instruction in composing ornamental chorales. And a work like "Ach Herr, mich armen Sünder," BWV 742, an ornamental setting with an essentially chordal accompaniment, might even be a direct product of this study period. On the whole, though, the accompanimental voices of Bach's earliest ornamental chorales have common motives (see, for instance, "Herr Jesu Christ, dich zu uns wend," BWV 709, and the *Orgelbüchlein* settings of "Das alte Jahr vergangen ist" and "Wenn wir in höchsten Nöten sein"). In the ornamental chorales from the Great Eighteen, the accompanimental voices tend to share common *themes*. And when Bach treats these themes in the manner of a ritornello, as will be discussed shortly, they acquire special significance.

Looking again at the accompaniment of this "Allein Gott" setting, we see that the right hand plays the embellished hymn tune only about half the time, a far smaller percentage than in Buxtehude's ornamental settings. In other words, the passages that contain nothing *but* accompaniment are considerably longer than in Buxtehude. One could make similar statements about almost any of the ornamental chorales from the Great Eighteen, which are among the longest in the organ repertory. In this collection, therefore, Bach also expands the ornamental chorale by lengthening the accompanimental introductions and interludes.

By far the longest of these passages is the introduction, which constitutes a full-blown fugal exposition in three voices, complete with a regular subject and countersubject. The fugal context is beyond doubt, despite the "premature" entrance of the alto and bass. Just observe how the first theme (the subject) appears successively in all three accompanimental voices, alternating between the tonic and dominant keys. (The theme is simplified in the bass at mm. 5–7 for the sake of pedaling.) An additional model for this intriguing piece, therefore, is fugue, that most standard of organ genres and probably one of the first in which Bach composed.

Equally compelling is our third ornamental chorale, the first of three settings of the Advent hymn "Nun komm, der Heiden Heiland." Since this work employs the same type of decorative passagework as the previous piece, Zehnder also dates it as 1711–13. This arrangement likewise draws from diverse sources. Whereas Bach may have cribbed its ornamental style from his Italian colleagues, he concludes by quoting a fellow German. Surely it cannot be happenstance that Buxtehude's ornamental setting of this same chorale also features a dramatic octave leap on g in the right hand exactly where the final pedal point begins, accompanied by the same parallel thirds in the left hand, and followed by a move toward the subdominant (see Examples 1-4 and 1-5). In both works, moreover, the embellishment from this point on is at its most profuse—standard north-German practice—allowing for a final, climactic flourish.[15]

This final surge is also the reason that the last ornamental phrase in both settings is the longest. Buxtehude otherwise sticks to four-bar phrases, allotting a half note's value to each note of the chorale tune. Bach begins each of his phrases as if it would last about two bars, at the rate of a quarter note for each chorale note. All four phrases end up, however, being two to three times this long. In this respect, Bach's setting again suggests the influence of Georg Böhm.

This work's pedal line, however, has no precedent in organ music. It represents the only instance of a true "walking-bass" pedal in any of

EXAMPLE 1-4. Dietrich Buxtehude, "Nun komm, der Heiden Heiland,"
BuxWV 211

EXAMPLE 1-5. "Nun komm, der Heiden Heiland," BWV 659a

Bach's organ chorales. (A walking bass is characterized by constant
stepwise motion in a note value half that of the main pulse.) He certainly hints at this type of pedal in the *Orgelbüchlein*.[16] But there the
"walking" tends to last only a few measures before being interrupted
by a long cadential note or, as in the case of "Ich ruf zu dir, Herr Jesu
Christ," the line consists largely of repeated notes. In the present composition, the pedal moves for the most part by step and for up to nine
measures at a time. It is a constant presence. Here, then, Bach unifies
his accompaniment not with common themes or motives but with a
common type of bass figuration.

Without question, the walking bass also enhances the Italian flavor
of Bach's recipe, for it is every bit as Italianate as the ornamentation

within the soprano line. Such bass lines do not regularly appear in music history until the sonatas and concertos of the late seventeenth-century Italian violin school, most notably those of Arcangelo Corelli and Giuseppe Torelli. Both the soprano and bass figuration of Bach's work seem especially close to the ornamental slow movements of Corelli's Opus 5 violin sonatas.

A further ornamental chorale from the Great Eighteen is the famous setting of "Schmücke dich, o liebe Seele." With its multitude of *agréments*, this work signals a return to French ornamental style. Still, due primarily to its accompanimental style, Zehnder dates the piece slightly later than the two previous settings. What is different about the accompaniment of "Schmücke dich" is that this is the first piece in our coverage to approach ritornello form, the standard design of late Baroque arias and concerto movements. The premise of this form, as is well known, is a recurring theme (called the ritornello) played by the accompanying orchestra at the beginning of the movement, prior to the soloist's entrance; several times during the movement, while the soloist is silent; and at the end of the movement, following the soloist's last appearance. In a chorale-ritornello movement, the individual phrases of the hymn tune normally take the place of the soloist's passages, and the phrases are separated by statements of the ritornello.

Georg Böhm is recognized as the first composer to write chorale-ritornello movements for organ, which suggests that he might once again have been Bach's model. Nowhere in the Great Eighteen, however, does Bach utilize Böhm's standard ritornello type, which is really nothing more than a long sequence. Instead, Bach fashions his ritornellos primarily after the initial chorale phrase. When he uses supplementary melodic models, as we will discuss later, he draws from the Italian concerto repertory.

The ritornello of "Schmücke dich" appears whole only at the outset. Nor does it return after the last chorale phrase, since the last note of this phrase is held to the very end, like most of Bach's chorale-ritornello settings for organ (and like most Baroque organ chorales in general). Yet portions of the theme are found in all the interludes, and during the final interlude the opening four measures are recapitulated twice.

In the previously discussed setting of "Allein Gott," nothing of this sort occurs. There the initial accompanimental idea—the fugue subject—returns in no interlude beyond the note-for-note repeat of the *Stollen*. True, the accompaniment of this work derives much of its material from the same two themes. But with the opening theme completely absent from the interludes during the second half of the piece, it seems inappropriate to speak of a "ritornello." What is more, the interludes of this work adhere strictly to the keys dictated by the hymn tune; those in "Schmücke dich" venture far beyond. Note especially the emphatic cadences in F minor in measures 22–23, before a chorale phrase in E-flat major, and in A-flat major in measures 98–99, before a chorale phrase in F minor.[17] Just as in a concerto movement or da capo aria, Bach's ritornello carves out new key areas before ultimately, in the final ritornello statement, reprising both the tonic key and the opening melodic material (m. 116).

With regard to its modulatory ritornello form, "Schmücke dich" displays a number of strong similarities to cantatas by Bach from 1714–16. But its extremely close correspondence to Cantata 199, *Mein Herze schwimmt im Blut*, suggests a slightly earlier composition date. Written in the summer of 1713,[18] the cantata includes a soprano aria, "Tief gebückt und voller Reue," in E-flat and in $\frac{3}{4}$ time whose ritornello begins with basically the same material as the organ chorale. For the first four bars, the bass lines are practically identical, the soprano lines share the same contour and several of the same pitches, and the harmonies are extremely similar as well (see Examples 1-6 and 1-7). All this leads Zehnder to assign "Schmücke dich" to 1712–14.

Issues of chronology aside—and Italian influence notwithstanding—"Schmücke dich" also projects a distinctly French facade, for it, too, is a kind of sarabande. The work possesses all the traits of the sarabande as the ornamental "Komm, Heiliger Geist" does, and its relatively homophonic texture and downbeat start align it even more closely with that dance type. Again, Bach's approach to composition is synthetic as well as international: he sets a German chorale simultaneously as a French dance and Italian ritornello movement.

A fifth ornamental chorale from the Great Eighteen is "An Wasserflüssen Babylon." In contrast to the previous ornamental settings, the embellished hymn tune here sounds not in the soprano but in the tenor voice, played on a separate manual.[19] This disposition, plus the numerous *agréments*—realized only in the late version—and relatively slow rhythms in the accompanimental voices, gives "An Wasserflüssen" the character of a *Tierce en Taille* (literally, "the Tierce stop in the tenor"). In this movement type, a standard item in French Baroque organ collections, the left hand plays an ornamental line on its own manual. And, yes, this work, too, is a sarabande, more so than any in the collection. It exemplifies all the traits of that dance type cited earlier, save homophonic texture, but it also favors four-bar phrases, the sine qua non of all dance music. All the chorale phrases except the last are of this length, and the ritornello that Bach employs consists of two such phrases.

EXAMPLE 1-6. Aria "Tief gebückt und voller Reue," from *Mein Herze schwimmt im Blut*, BWV 199. Piano reduction by Max Schneider, Edition Breitkopf 7199. Breitkopf & Härtel, Wiesbaden—Leipzig. Used by permission.

EXAMPLE 1-7. "Schmücke dich, o liebe Seele," BWV 654a

At first blush, this ritornello appears to be only seven bars long, since the embellished chorale tune enters in measure 7. Actually, though, the ritornello overlaps with the first chorale phrase for two bars and does not end until the tonic triad on the downbeat of measure 8. Throughout the piece, both phrases of the ritornello appear often enough, either as interludes or simultaneously with the embellished chorale, to suggest an ostinato. As in "Schmücke dich," the final ritornello statement brings back the opening phrase in the home key. In terms of compositional models, then, "An Wasserflüssen" is our most complex work yet. It is at once a *Tierce en Taille*, a sarabande, a ritornello movement, and an ornamental chorale.

The close affinity of this remarkable piece to "Schmücke dich" (sarabande traits, ritornello form) suggests that "An Wasserflüssen" may also have originated between 1712 and 1714. It was around this same time that Bach copied out Nicholas de Grigny's *Premier livre d'orgue*,[20] a collection whose *Tierce en Taille* is the most celebrated in the whole organ repertory. Was this movement a factor in Bach's thinking?

THE CANTUS FIRMUS CHORALE

In a cantus firmus chorale, the entire hymn tune appears in long notes, like a cantus firmus in a Renaissance mass. The chorale tune is normally stated in half notes, with accompanimental figuration in eighth or sixteenth notes. But if the accompanimental parts consist largely of sixteenths or thirty-seconds, the melody may be written in quarter notes and still give the same "sustained" effect. The tune usually sounds in the soprano or bass, with little or no ornamentation, and with interludes between phrases.

Although movements in this style are common in the chorale partitas of Sweelinck and his pupil Scheidt, the central-German master Johann Pachelbel (1653–1706) was the first to establish the cantus firmus chorale as a standard design for works in only one movement. About fifty such works by Pachelbel survive, mostly in three voices.[21] As well as being the most prolific composer of cantus firmus chorales for organ, Pachelbel crystallized the form through the use of pre-imitation for some or all of the chorale phrases. According to this technique, before a phrase of the chorale is stated in long notes by one of the outer voices, it is the subject of imitation in the other parts, in rhythms either two or four times as fast. Otherwise, Pachelbel's accompaniment consists of little more than running parts that lack any thematic or motivic unity.

By the turn of the eighteenth century, the Pachelbel type of cantus firmus chorale was a standard chorale form in central Germany, cultivated by the likes of Andreas Armsdorff, J. M. Bach, Christian Friedrich Witte, and (Handel's teacher) Friedrich Wilhelm Zachow, as well as by Pachelbel's pupils Johann Heinrich Buttstedt and Andreas Nicolaus Vetter. Buttstedt, in turn, passed the design on to his pupil (and J. S. Bach's kinsman) J. G. Walther.

Another of Pachelbel's students was Sebastian Bach's older brother and keyboard instructor, Johann Christoph Bach (1671–1721). In 1695, after having lost both of his parents, the nine-year-old Sebastian moved to Ohrdruf to live under this sibling's roof and remained there until 1700. During these five years, Christoph probably taught the boy everything from keyboard playing to organ maintenance and repair. None of Christoph's own compositions are extant. One can well imagine, though, that he schooled his younger brother in the forms taught to him by his teacher Pachelbel, including of course the cantus firmus chorale. Since two cantus firmus chorales by J. S. Bach ("Christe, der du bist Tag und Licht" and "Wie nach einer Wasserquelle") are preserved in the Neumeister Collection, which evidently contains Bach's earliest works of any kind, he appears to have adopted this form very early on. That he also employed it at a rather late date is attested to by the presence of five such works in Part III of the *Clavierübung*, published in 1739.

The Great Eighteen contain five cantus firmus chorales proper. "Nun danket alle Gott" and "Vor deinen Thron tret ich hiermit" are both clear-cut specimens of the Pachelbel type in their use of pre-imitation for all phrases of the chorale tune, which is stated in both works by the soprano voice. (In "Vor deinen Thron," however, the hymn melody moves twice as fast as one would expect in a cantus firmus chorale.) Still, Bach easily surpasses this model in several respects. He strictly maintains four, not three, voices; he varies his imitative writing through the use of stretto, augmentation, diminution, and inversion; and he develops and unifies his accompanimental voices in general to a far greater extent by means of common motives.

The composition date of "Vor deinen Thron" is a complex—even mysterious—matter best understood in conjunction with the autograph manuscript of the Great Eighteen. We will therefore revisit this issue in the next chapter. As for "Nun danket," Zehnder has pointed out that the chorale setting "Jesu, deine Passion" from Bach's Weimar cantata *Himmelskönig, sei willkommen*, BWV 182, also represents the Pachelbel type of cantus firmus chorale, with pre-imitation of all the chorale phrases and a soprano cantus firmus to boot. Since the cantata dates from 1714, perhaps the organ chorale does as well.

The other cantus firmus chorales from the Great Eighteen include the famous "fantasy" on the Pentecost hymn "Komm, Heiliger Geist, Herre Gott"; the third and final setting of "Nun komm, der Heiden Heiland"; and "Von Gott will ich nicht lassen." In these arrangements, Pachelbel's style is abandoned in favor of a more synthetic design, one that incorporates the genres of fugue and concerto. As in the ornamental chorales from the Great Eighteen, this fusion of genres allows Bach to unify and expand his accompanimental material well beyond anything that earlier composers of cantus firmus chorales could have dreamed. And he makes this material so compelling that the presentation of the hymn tune seems almost incidental.

The first two of these works are as close as any in the collection. They are the only settings designated by Bach in the autograph manuscript as *in organo pleno* ("for full organ"). In each, the chorale melody appears in the bass voice (played on the pedals), while the upper three parts comprise a fugue whose subject derives from the first phrase of the chorale. Both pieces also display tendencies of ritornello form in conjunction with perpetual sixteenth-note motion.

We have already established that the ornamental setting of "Allein Gott" begins with a fugal exposition. In that work, however, as soon as the embellished hymn melody enters, the fugue ends. Although the accompanimental voices continue to refer to the fugue's subject and countersubject, they never again do so in a fugal context. The composer of a fugue may have carte blanche beyond the opening exposition. But the form, at least according to the Bachian model, typically continues with many more imitative statements of the subject in various keys, sometimes involving such devices as inversion, augmentation, and stretto. One searches in vain for anything of this ilk in the "Allein Gott" arrangement.

The two works presently under consideration, conversely, illustrate almost every aspect of this scheme. In both, the initial exposition (which in "Komm, Heiliger Geist" is disguised by a pedal point) is followed by several imitative statements of the subject in different keys; some of these statements, furthermore, are inverted. The "Nun komm" setting even features a stretto statement of the inverted and upright forms of its subject, timed to coincide with the final pedal entrance.

There is no denying, either, that both works are also ritornello movements. As in the ornamental settings of "Schmücke dich" and "An Wasserflüssen Babylon," the same theme (the fugue subject) presents itself in all the interludes and often in keys not governed by the chorale melody. But "Komm, Heiliger Geist" and "Nun komm" are even more unified than these two works through their constant surface motion in sixteenth notes—a feature of the fugue subjects themselves—which imparts to the music a strong sense of rhythmic drive.

It is hard not to view this combination of ritornello form and perpetual motion in connection with the concertos of Antonio Vivaldi. Bach evidently got acquainted with these works in 1713, after Prince Johann Ernst of Weimar had sent to the Weimar court a large quantity of music—presumably including Vivaldi's *L'Estro Armonico* concertos—bought during his stay in the Netherlands.[22] During the next few years, until he left Weimar in 1717, Bach made organ transcriptions of some of these concertos (see BWV 593, 594, and 596) and began to assimilate Vivaldi's concerto style into his own vocal and instrumental compositions. Two organ works presumably from this period are the Toccata in F Major, BWV 540/1, and the "Dorian" Toccata, BWV 538/1. Both are ritornello movements that open with a triad-oriented theme in continuous sixteenths, one of Vivaldi's favorite melodic types (see Examples 1-8 and 1-9).[23]

Significantly, the ritornello themes of our two organ chorales are cut from the same cloth, with arpeggiation of the tonic and leading-tone seventh chords in "Komm, Heiliger Geist," and tonic and dominant triads in "Nun komm" (see Examples 1-10 and 1-11). In fact, the ritor-

EXAMPLE 1-8. Toccata in F Major, BWV 540/1

EXAMPLE 1-9. Toccata in D Minor (Dorian), BWV 538/1

nello of the "Nun komm" arrangement employs the same four-note head motive as the two toccatas. "Komm, Heiliger Geist," meanwhile, opens with exactly the same texture—and in the same key—as the F-major toccata: imitative writing in two parts above a low F pedal point.

When might Bach have composed these two chorale settings? Certainly during his years of "Vivaldi fever," 1713–17, but most likely around 1714. For in the penultimate movement of Cantata 172, *Erschallet, ihr Lieder, erklinget, ihr Saiten*, written for Pentecost Sunday 1714, Bach treats the chorale "Komm, Heiliger Geist, Herre Gott" in the same highly exceptional way as in our organ setting: instead of setting all ten phrases of this unusually long melody, he omits the fourth, fifth, sixth, and seventh phrases.[24] Considering the extremely close similarities between this organ chorale and the "Nun komm" arrangement, one can tentatively assign the latter work to 1714 as well.

Like these two settings, the remaining cantus firmus chorale from the Great Eighteen, "Von Gott will ich nicht lassen," contains a ritornello in imitative (though not fugal) texture, with the hymn tune played on the pedals. (Here, though, the pedals represent the tenor voice, and the bottom manual part the bass, as in the *pedaliter* settings of "Christ, unser Herr, zum Jordan kam" and "Jesus Christus, unser Heiland" from Part III of the *Clavierübung*). It may also date from 1714.

EXAMPLE 1-10. "Komm, Heiliger Geist, Herre Gott," BWV 651a

EXAMPLE 1-11. "Nun komm, der Heiden Heiland," BWV 661a

THE CHORALE TRIO

Associated with central Germany, the chorale trio is a three-voice set-ting in which the upper two parts are played on separate manuals and the bottom voice on the pedals. Throughout the late seventeenth and early eighteenth centuries, composers such as Pachelbel, Zachow, Armsdorff, and Walther frequently employed this disposition for cantus firmus chorales, with one voice stating the entire chorale tune in long notes. That Bach composed such works himself is evinced by the miscellaneous settings of "Wo soll ich fliehen hin," BWV 694, "Wir Christenleut," BWV 710, and "Nun freut euch, lieben Christen g'mein," BWV 734, as well as the *pedaliter* setting of "Jesus Christus, unser Heiland" from Part III of the *Clavierübung*. In the Great Eighteen chorales, though, he elevated the chorale trio far beyond the status of a texture to a legitimate chorale type, one that openly simulated the fast movements of contemporary Italian trio sonatas and concertos. As Werner Breig has maintained, this thoroughly modern design may well represent Bach's single greatest innovation to the genre of the organ chorale.[25]

Arguably the most progressive chorale trios from the Great Eighteen—and possibly the most forward-looking pieces in the entire collection—are "Herr Jesu Christ, dich zu uns wend" and the third setting of "Allein Gott in der Höh sei Ehr." Both works adopt the same idiosyncratic design, which joins a ritornello form to a cantus firmus chorale. In each, the ritornello theme is stated initially in imitative texture. (The "Allein Gott" setting commences, remarkably, with a total of six fugal statements of its ritornello.) Following the last of these imitative statements, where the listener expects the first phrase of the chorale proper, free episodic material appears instead. This new material leads to a modulation, after which the ritornello resurfaces in the new key. For roughly the next fifty measures of each piece, statements of the ritornello in various keys alternate with free material. Only at the very end does the chorale melody proper sound (as a pedal part), in sustained notes. In "Herr Jesu Christ," the entire melody is given; in the "Allein Gott" setting, only the first two phrases.

Clearly, the main difference between this type of ritornello form and that encountered elsewhere in the Great Eighteen is the music that occurs between the statements of the ritornello: by inserting free material instead of the successive phrases of the chorale, Bach devises a scheme that comes infinitely closer to Italian instrumental music of his day. He is not in any way bound by the chorale melody or its harmonic implications but is able to modulate to any key and to offer as many statements of the ritornello as he wishes. Since he is content merely, in the ritornello theme, to paraphrase the tune or, in the free episodes, to ignore it, the music sounds less like a chorale setting than a movement from a trio sonata (three-voice texture) or concerto (ritornello form with free episodes).[26] Both manual parts are also in the treble register, like the vast majority of Baroque trio sonatas. With respect to texture, form, range, and figuration, the parallels to Bach's six trio sonatas for organ are clear.

Zehnder argues convincingly that the specific Italian models for these two works and several others from Bach's Weimar period include the Opus 8 concertos of Giuseppe Torelli, published posthumously in 1709. Bach may have gotten to know this collection—a watershed in the history of the concerto—through Torelli's student Johann Georg Pisendel, who visited Weimar in 1709. At any rate, Walther's organ transcriptions of two concertos from this opus document its reception in Weimar. That Bach himself studied Torelli's music is attested to by his keyboard arrangement of one of Torelli's concertos (BWV 979), probably also prepared in Weimar.

In "Herr Jesu Christ," the style of Torelli's Opus 8 asserts itself in different ways, including the type of figuration used. But the Italian's influence is most evident in the extreme brevity of the ritornello, which is only one bar long, and the key scheme of I–V–vi–iii employed for its first four statements. Such a concise melody is far removed from the long, segmented ritornello themes favored by Vivaldi and other concerto composers of the time. The key sequence, too, with its distinctive pairing of ritornello statements according to mode (major-major followed by minor-minor), differs from Vivaldi's practice. Of Bach's Weimar compositions that employ similarly short ritornello themes, only two are securely datable: the "Hunting" cantata, *Was mir behagt, ist nur die muntre Jagd!*, BWV 208, from 1712 or 1713; and Cantata 182, *Himmelskönig, sei willkommen*, composed for Palm Sunday 1714. This leads Zehnder to date "Herr Jesu Christ" as 1712–14.

Because of its many close similarities to "Herr Jesu Christ," the setting of "Allein Gott" probably also originated during these years. This work employs neither Torelli's type of ritornello nor his unusual modulation pattern. Instead, it follows his technique of using the same material for two or more solo episodes within one movement. In the organ chorale, the first and third episodes (mm. 35–43 and 56–64) contain the same music, as do the second and fourth (mm. 46–56 and 67–79). Zehnder shows that much of this chorale's figuration also bears Torelli's stamp. But it would be hard to deny the influence of Vivaldi in a passage such as Example 1-12, whose pedal motive is a veritable cliché of his. Just think of how Vivaldi begins the slow movement of his A-minor concerto, op. 3, no. 8, as transcribed for organ by Bach (see Example 1-13).

Another of the Great Eighteen chorales that we should take up here is the second setting of "Allein Gott in der Höh sei Ehr." Despite its free voice leading, which sometimes encompasses five parts, Bach

EXAMPLE 1-12. "Allein Gott in der Höh sei Ehr," BWV 664a

EXAMPLE 1-13. Bach-Vivaldi, Adagio from Concerto in A Minor, BWV 593

scores this work primarily for three parts, with each hand taking its own part, frequently on its own manual. Thus, the piece has the unmistakable sound and palpable feel of a chorale trio. For the first fourteen bars, it proceeds similarly to the third setting of this hymn, just discussed. A lively ritornello theme appears in the top voice, accompanied by a slower countermelody in the pedals, and moves successively to the alto (left hand) and bass (pedals). These two melodies also have roughly the same shape as those in the third "Allein Gott" setting. As the texture thickens to three parts, a fugal exposition occurs. And yet the hands remain on the same manual. Only after the opening fugal passage is a second keyboard engaged, for the phrase-by-phrase presentation of the chorale tune in the tenor register, in a highly embellished form. This last feature means, of course, that this work is also a clear-cut example of an ornamental chorale. Zehnder hazards no guess about a composition date. But considering its trio orientation and close analogies to the third "Allein Gott" setting, why could this piece not have originated at about the same time as the previous two?

A final chorale trio from the Great Eighteen is the second setting of "Nun komm, der Heiden Heiland." In terms of compositional models, this arrangement ranks as one of the more interesting in the whole collection. It, too, represents an ornamental chorale in ritornello form. In other significant respects, though, the piece breaks new ground. For one thing, it is Bach's only trio—of any sort—with the inverted disposition of one treble and two bass lines (in accordance with the composer's own subtitle, "a due Bassi"). The feet and left hand combine to spin out a ritornello theme, while the right hand plays the embellished hymn tune. Although Bach could have devised this scoring entirely on his own, models were certainly available, from his native Germany and elsewhere. Take, for instance, Buxtehude's trio sonatas for violin, gamba, and continuo or the trio sonatas for one treble and two bass parts by Giovanni Legrenzi.[27] Bach's knowledge of this Italian's music is documented by the Fugue in C Minor, BWV 574, which is based on a theme by Legrenzi.

But a more tangible influence is that, once again, of Antonio Vivaldi, for here is the only Great Eighteen chorale that employs Vivaldi's patented ritornello formula. This is a type of ritornello, appropriated by Bach on so many occasions, that consists of three clearly differentiated and easily separated segments, each of which has its own function. The first segment grounds the tonality with mostly tonic and dominant harmonies, ending usually on the dominant; the second entails a sequence whose chords progress in the order of descending fifths; and the third concludes the theme with a satisfying dominant-tonic cadence. In the ritornello of his organ chorale, Bach follows this syntax to the letter (see Example 1-14). The first segment (mm. 1–3), once it moves beyond the chorale tune, alternates between tonic and dominant harmonies, concluding on the dominant; the second (mm. 4–5) forms a textbook circle-of-fifths sequence (and adopts such additional Vivaldian traits as motoric sixteenth notes and triadic contours); and the third (mm. 6–7) brings things to a close with an authentic cadence.

Regarding Bach's use of canon for the first three measures of his ritornello, one might assume this was the master contrapuntist's way of grafting his own style onto an otherwise "foreign" design. But Vivaldi was no stranger to this technique. Two of his most famous concertos open with canons, and both of them were transcribed for organ by Bach (BWV 594 and 596). The latter transcription, that of the D-minor concerto, op. 3, no. 11, even begins, like our organ chorale, in trio texture and with canonic writing at the unison in the tenor and bass registers.

In light of this connection, it may be significant that Bach's autograph manuscript of this transcription originated during 1714–17, since this is also the date of his autograph of the early version of this organ chorale.[28] Because the latter is not a composing score, even though it contains compositional revisions, this dating means only that 1717 is the latest possible year of composition. Considering Vivaldi's profound impact on the work, it can scarcely date from before 1713. Zehnder's

EXAMPLE 1-14. "Nun komm, der Heiden Heiland," BWV 660a

findings indicate that Bach did not begin writing "Vivaldian" ritornellos until his church cantatas of 1715–16, suggesting that this chorale
setting also stems from these years. If so, the trio on "Nun komm" was
one of the last of the Great Eighteen chorales to be composed.

The conclusions of this chapter are summarized in Table 1-1. It indicates that Bach followed no fewer than a dozen different models in composing the Great Eighteen. This table also lists the works in roughly
chronological order. If our chronology is correct, the composition of the
these extraordinary pieces involved Bach intermittently throughout his
Weimar tenure (1708–17). Certain settings appear to be from the beginning of this period (or even as early as 1707, while Bach was in
Mühlhausen), others from the middle, and at least one (the "Nun komm"
trio) from the end.

   During this time, Bach's overall compositional style changed dramatically due to his encounter with contemporary Italian music, particularly that of Vivaldi. Indeed, Bach's assimilation of this repertory

TABLE 1-1 The Compositional Models of the Great Eighteen Chorales, according to the Early Versions

BWV No.	Title	Chorale Type(s)	Other Model(s)	Proposed Composition Date
665a	"Jesus Christus, unser Heiland"	chorale motet		1707–8
666a	"Jesus Christus, unser Heiland"	chorale motet		1707–8
652a	"Komm, Heiliger Geist, Herre Gott"	chorale motet ornamental chorale	sarabande	1707–8
656a	"O Lamm Gottes, unschuldig"	chorale partita		1707–8
667a	"Komm, Gott Schöpfer, Heiliger Geist"	chorale partita		1709–17
662a	"Allein Gott in der Höh sei Ehr"	ornamental chorale	Italian violin music fugue	1711–13
659a	"Nun komm, der Heiden Heiland"	ornamental chorale	Italian violin music	1711–13
654a	"Schmücke dich, o liebe Seele"	ornamental chorale	sarabande ritornello form	1712–14
653a	"An Wasserflüssen Babylon"	ornamental chorale	sarabande *Tierce en Taille* ritornello form	1712–14
657a	"Nun danket alle Gott"	cantus firmus chorale		1714
651a	"Komm, Heiliger Geist, Herre Gott"	cantus firmus chorale	fugue Vivaldi's concertos	1714
661a	"Nun komm, der Heiden Heiland"	cantus firmus chorale	fugue Vivaldi's concertos	1714
658a	"Von Gott will ich nicht lassen"	cantus firmus chorale	ritornello form	1714

BWV No.	Title	Chorale Type(s)	Other Model(s)	Proposed Composition Date
655a	"Herr Jesu Christ, dich zu uns wend"	chorale trio cantus firmus chorale	ritornello form Italian instrumental music	1712–14
664a	"Allein Gott in der Höh sei Ehr"	chorale trio cantus firmus chorale	ritornello form Italian instrumental music fugue	1712–14
663a	"Allein Gott in der Höh sei Ehr"	ornamental chorale chorale trio	ritornello form fugue	1712–14
660a	"Nun komm, der Heiden Heiland"	ornamental chorale chorale trio	ritornello form Vivaldi's concertos	1715–16

during the latter half of his Weimar period represents the single most critical development toward the formation of his own personal style, a style whose basis is the blending of Italianisms with complex polyphony.[29] The Great Eighteen chorales, as tabulated here, clearly represent a case study of this process. The earliest settings tend also to be the most simple and conventional: for the most part, they adopt only one model, and that a chorale type. The remaining works take a decidedly eclectic approach to chorale composition, one that relies heavily on Italian models.

But our emphasis here has been less on chronology than on Bach's compositional exemplars and the many musical issues they raise. Their sheer variety is astonishing, as is the composer's uncanny ability to adapt them all to the narrow confines of a chorale setting. To study the models for the Great Eighteen, therefore, is to learn about not only the Baroque organ chorale but also Baroque music in general.

Chapter 2

THE GENESIS OF THE COLLECTION

One often reads that the Great Eighteen originated as independent works. While this remains an unproven assumption, we have no reason to doubt it. There is no evidence whatever that these pieces constituted a collection of any kind until late in Bach's life.

When, in 1717, Bach left Weimar to become *Kapellmeister* in Cöthen, his baggage must have included the (lost) autograph manuscripts of the early versions of the Great Eighteen chorales. His new position did not oblige him to compose for or even play the organ, but this does not necessarily mean that during his six years in Cöthen Bach left the Great Eighteen untouched. Among other things, he may have taught some of the pieces to his private keyboard pupils there, as he appears to have done with the *Orgelbüchlein*.

In 1723, Bach moved from Cöthen to the city of Leipzig. Here he was cantor at St. Thomas and municipal director of music, a title he held until his death in 1750. This post did not entail the production of organ music, either. Indeed, the only hard evidence of Bach's involvement with the Great Eighteen chorales from the beginning of his Leipzig tenure to around 1740 is a manuscript copy of the first setting of "Allein Gott" (early version) by Bach's pupil Heinrich Nicolaus Gerber. Gerber presumably prepared this source in Leipzig around 1725, under Bach's direct supervision.[1]

THE AUTOGRAPH MANUSCRIPT

That Bach began around 1740 to compile the Great Eighteen into a collection is documented by the autograph manuscript of the set. Housed today in the Staatsbibliothek zu Berlin under the shelf number P 271, this source also contains the autographs of the Canonic Variations on "Vom Himmel hoch" and the six trio sonatas for organ.[2] Since the autographs of most of Bach's organ works have not survived, this ranks as one of the most important sources altogether for this repertory.

It actually consists of three separate manuscripts that date from various times in Bach's life. In their order of appearance, they are (1) the autograph of the trio sonatas, from 1727–32; (2) the autograph of the Great Eighteen and Canonic Variations, from circa 1739–50; and (3) the autograph of the early version of the trio on "Nun komm" from the Great Eighteen, from 1714–17.[3] At some point, either Bach himself or one of his heirs bound the first two manuscripts together. Sometime later, after Bach's death, the third manuscript was appended to this bound volume, but by whom is unclear.

For obvious reasons, we will focus here on the second of these sources. Unlike the other two, it is not entirely autograph. It begins with the first fifteen of the Great Eighteen chorales in Bach's hand, followed by the sixteenth and seventeenth chorales in the hand of Johann Christoph Altnikol, a pupil of Bach in Leipzig from 1744 to 1748. The Canonic Variations appear next, in Bach's hand, followed by the eighteenth chorale in the hand of an anonymous scribe (see Table 2-1).

In his groundbreaking research on Bach's handwriting, undertaken in the 1950s, Georg von Dadelsen dated all of Bach's entries in this source between circa 1744 and 1748.[4] Dadelsen also maintained that the entries of the fourteenth and fifteenth chorales originated at a distinctly later time within this period than the first thirteen. Relying on documents unavailable to Dadelsen, Yoshitake Kobayashi has recently demonstrated that Bach notated the first thirteen chorales somewhat earlier, around 1739–42, and the fourteenth and fifteenth chorales around 1746–47.[5] Thus, Bach began to compile the Great Eighteen shortly after completing Part III of the *Clavierübung*, published in 1739. As we will discuss in the next chapter, he probably also regarded the two from a musical perspective as complementary collections.

The changes in Bach's handwriting that led Dadelsen and Kobayashi to assign the fourteenth and fifteenth chorales to a later time are illustrated in Figure 2-1. This page of the autograph begins with the last measures of the second setting of "Allein Gott," notated between circa 1739 and 1742, and continues with the opening bars of the third

TABLE 2-1 The Contents of the Autograph Manuscript

BWV No.	Title	Foliation	Scribe	Date of Entry
		f. 1^r (blank page)		
651	"Komm, Heiliger Geist, Herre Gott"	f. 1^v–3^r	Bach	ca. 1739–42
652	"Komm, Heiliger Geist, Herre Gott"	f. 3^v–5^v	Bach	ca. 1739–42
653	"An Wasserflüssen Babylon"	f. 5^v–6^v	Bach	ca. 1739–42
654	"Schmücke dich, o liebe Seele"	f. 6^v–7^v	Bach	ca. 1739–42
655	"Herr Jesu Christ, dich zu uns wend"	f. 7^v–9^r	Bach	ca. 1739–42
656	"O Lamm Gottes, unschuldig"	f. 9^r–10^r	Bach	ca. 1739–42
657	"Nun danket alle Gott"	f. 10^v–11^r	Bach	ca. 1739–42
658	"Von Gott will ich nicht lassen"	f. 11^v–12^r	Bach	ca. 1739–42
659	"Nun komm, der Heiden Heiland"	f. 12^r–13^r	Bach	ca. 1739–42
660	"Nun komm, der Heiden Heiland"	f. 13^r–13^v	Bach	ca. 1739–42
661	"Nun komm, der Heiden Heiland"	f. 13^v–14^v	Bach	ca. 1739–42
662	"Allein Gott in der Höh sei Ehr"	f. 15^r–15^v	Bach	ca. 1739–42
663	"Allein Gott in der Höh sei Ehr"	f. 15^v–17^v	Bach	ca. 1739–42
664	"Allein Gott in der Höh sei Ehr"	f. 17^v–19^r	Bach	ca. 1746–47
665	"Jesus Christus, unser Heiland"	f. 19^v–20^r	Bach	ca. 1746–47
666	"Jesus Christus, unser Heiland"	f. 20^v–21^r	Altnikol	August 1750– April 1751
667	"Komm, Gott Schöpfer, Heiliger Geist"	f. 21^v–22^r	Altnikol	August 1750– April 1751
769a	Canonic Variations on "Vom Himmel hoch"	f. 22^v–25^v	Bach	ca. 1747–48
668	"Vor deinen Thron tret ich hiermit" (incomplete)	f. 25^v	anonymous copyist	April–July 1750
		f. 26 (lost)		

FIGURE 2-1. Autograph score of "Allein Gott in der Höh sei Ehr," BWV 663,
mm. 120–27; and "Allein Gott in der Höh sei Ehr," BWV 664, mm. 1–16
(Staatsbibliothek zu Berlin—Preussischer Kulturbesitz, Musikabteilung mit
Mendelssohn-Archiv, Mus. ms. Bach P 271, p. 90)

setting, entered about four years later. (Since most of the first fifteen chorales overlap in this way, it is obvious that all of them were notated in their order of appearance.) Generally speaking, Bach's hand in the earlier entry tends to slant somewhat to the right, as opposed to the more vertical (and smaller) script of the later entry. Differences also exist with respect to particular symbols. A glance at the second, third, and fourth systems, for instance, reveals that the quarter rests of the earlier entry are relatively ornate. Most telling are the half notes with downward stems, which in the earlier entry have oval note heads with stems on the left and in the later entry have rounder note heads (which are sometimes open at the top) with stems in the middle.

Bach's entry of the fifteenth chorale is followed on the next four pages by Altnikol's entries of the sixteenth and seventeenth chorales. The next seven pages contain Bach's entry of the Canonic Variations. This work was published in 1747, to commemorate Bach's induction in June of that year into Lorenz Mizler's Society of the Musical Sciences. The published version (BWV 769) is clearly earlier than that found in the autograph (BWV 769a), which implies that the latter version did not originate before 1747. To judge from Bach's script, he entered this version into the autograph in either 1747 or 1748.[6]

To return to Altnikol, his presence in this manuscript raises a host of questions. Scholars have traditionally assumed that his two entries predate Bach's entry of the Canonic Variations, and this theory agrees with both Kobayashi's redating of the autograph and the time frame of Altnikol's study with Bach. The composer could have instructed his pupil to add these two compositions to the fifteen he had already notated.

Why, however, would Bach have entrusted this task to a student when he could have entered both works himself? In preparing this manuscript, he was not laboring under any time constraints, such as a Sunday deadline, that would have necessitated outside help. Rather, he was taking time to inscribe these works in a remarkably legible and even calligraphic fashion and to revise the musical content of each and every one as well.

Moreover, recent investigations into Bach's musical estate imply that Altnikol could have entered both works sometime after Bach's death in 1750. For in 1749 Altnikol had married Bach's daughter Elisabeth Juliana Friederica, and there is reason to believe she inherited autograph manuscripts of her father's music.[7] If the autograph of the Great Eighteen was one of these, Altnikol had direct access to this source from 1750 until his death in 1759. Also suggestive in this regard is the fact that Bach's son Carl Philipp Emanuel Bach, at the time of his death in 1788, owned the autograph, as well as several of Altnikol's J. S. Bach copies.[8] He may have come into the possession of all these sources, through his sister, shortly after Altnikol's death.

Very recently, Peter Wollny has uncovered further evidence that points in this direction.[9] He has shown, first of all, that Altnikol's two entries in the autograph represent a different phase of his handwriting than do his Leipzig manuscripts that carry actual dates (1744 and 1748). Again, most revealing are the half notes with downward stems, which in the dated sources feature oval note heads with stems on the left or right. As can be seen in Figure 2-2, Altnikol's entry of the *manualiter* "Jesus Christus, unser Heiland," he draws these symbols in the autograph of the Great Eighteen with relatively large, round note heads and with stems in the middle.[10] Wollny also points out that the only Altnikol manuscripts that match his script in the Great Eighteen autograph are also partially in the hand of Bach's very last pupil, Johann Gottfried Müthel. During a year's leave of absence from the court at Schwerin, Müthel studied first with Bach in Leipzig from early May 1750 and then for a while with Altnikol in Naumburg. These jointly copied sources therefore could not have originated later than 1751. That they were prepared after Müthel left Leipzig—for Altnikol could have collaborated with him in Leipzig, say while visiting his sick father-in-law—is indicated by their watermarks, which are atypical of that city.

We may conclude, then, that Altnikol made his two entries in Naumburg between August 1750—Bach died on July 28—and April 1751. Along with Kobayashi's redating of the autograph, the likelihood that Altnikol's portions of the manuscript originated after Bach's death significantly changes our understanding of the Great Eighteen as a collection, since Altnikol apparently added the sixteenth and seventeenth chorales without the composer's authorization. (As we will discuss in the next chapter, this hypothesis also bears profound implications for the musical structure of the collection.) It follows that Bach left blank the four pages between the fifteenth chorale and the Canonic Variations simply as a means of separating the latter work—which is unquestionably an independent composition—from the preceding fifteen. Accordingly, Altnikol was careful in choosing two works of relatively modest size that would not exceed the available space. But size was obviously not the only criterion, since the first chorale he notated ("Jesus Christus, unser Heiland") is based on the same hymn as Bach's entry that precedes it.

The fragmentary eighteenth chorale is not in Bach's hand, either. This work appears on the very last page of the autograph, directly beneath the last system of Bach's entry of the Canonic Variations. For years it was believed that this piece, too, was entered by Altnikol. The early Bach bi-

FIGURE 2-2. Altnikol's entry of "Jesus Christus, unser Heiland," BWV 666, mm. 1–24 (Staatsbibliothek zu Berlin—Preussischer Kulturbesitz, Musikabteilung mit Mendelssohn-Archiv, Mus. ms. Bach P 271, p. 96)

35

ographer Johann Nicolaus Forkel, writing around 1800, even reported that Altnikol had copied down the work as dictated by Bach on his deathbed. This account was taken as holy writ—and made the stuff of legend—until Dadelsen's discovery that the scribe is actually an anonymous copyist (known in the Bach literature as "Anon. Vr") who also appears in the original performing parts of sacred vocal works by Bach from the 1740s.[11] Clearly, this individual belonged to Bach's Leipzig circle toward the end of the composer's life, and since his hand appears most often in continuo parts, he was probably an organist. His entry of the eighteenth chorale, "Vor deinen Thron," is found in Figure 2-3.

The compositional history of Bach's "deathbed" chorale, alas, is rather complicated. Its original version is the ornamental *Orgelbüchlein* chorale "Wenn wir in höchsten Nöten sein," BWV 641, composed evidently no later than 1713.[12] At some point, while he was still in Weimar or later, Bach removed the ornamentation from the soprano voice and added imitative passages before each phrase of the chorale, transforming the work into a cantus firmus chorale à la Pachelbel. This version of the piece, cataloged as BWV 668a, was appended to the original print of Bach's *Art of Fugue*, published posthumously in 1751, to compensate for the incompleteness of its final fugue. The fragmentary version of the chorale that appears in the autograph of the Great Eighteen, titled "Vor deinen Thron tret ich hiermit" (BWV 668), represents a slightly revised version of BWV 668a.

According to the original print of the *Art of Fugue*, probably edited by no less an authority than C. P. E. Bach, Sebastian Bach had dictated BWV 668a in his blindness "on the spur of the moment to the pen of one of his friends." Considering that Bach went blind sometime after his first unsuccessful eye operation at the end of March 1750, the anonymous scribe could have entered "Vor deinen Thron" no earlier than April 1750 and presumably sometime before Bach's death on July 28.

But this entry contains none of the revisions we might expect from a dictation score; it is a fair copy entirely free of corrections. And, as Christoph Wolff has observed, the notion of the blind composer flawlessly dictating an entire work written thirty years earlier is hard to fathom.[13] For even in his prime Bach did not rely solely on his memory. Whether he was preparing performing parts for a just-finished score or revising pieces composed decades earlier, he still used the original manuscripts as a guide. Bach's overall health at this time must also be taken into account, as recent research indicates he was suffering from untreated diabetes.[14]

Wolff proposes instead an eminently more credible scenario. At some point during Bach's last few months, the blind composer asks someone

FIGURE 2-3. Autograph score of Canonic Variations on "Vom Himmel hoch, da komm ich her," BWV 769a, final variation, mm. 38–42; and anonymous scribe's entry of "Vor deinen Thron tret ich hiermit," BWV 668 (Staatsbibliothek zu Berlin—Preussischer Kulturbesitz, Musikabteilung mit Mendelssohn-Archiv, Mus. ms. Bach P 271, p. 106)

to play for him his organ chorale "Wenn wir in höchsten Nöten sein," BWV 668a (a hymn whose title translates, so fittingly with regard to Bach's personal situation at the time, as "When We Are in the Greatest Distress"). Bach next dictates a number of revisions to the work, which an assistant—possibly the same person as our anonymous scribe—copies onto a now lost manuscript. With his thoughts turning increasingly to the hereafter, Bach renames the piece "Before Your Throne I Now Appear" and requests that it be added to the autograph of the Great Eighteen. Working from the lost manuscript, the anonymous scribe enters the revised version, BWV 668.

This entry breaks off at the very end of the last system of the page, in the middle of measure 26, and concludes with directs for the next beat (that indicate the same pitches found at this juncture in BWV 668a).[15] The fascicle structure of the manuscript shows beyond any doubt that this page was originally followed by another folio, which at some point became detached from the rest of the source. All indications are, then, that the scribe entered a complete copy of BWV 668, of which only the first half is extant. Unfortunately, no other source for this version of the work survives.

COMPOSITIONAL PROCESS

The contents of the autograph of the Great Eighteen—according to BWV number, work title, foliation, scribe, and date of entry—are summarized in Table 2-1. As we continue, let us observe how Bach compiled this manuscript from one piece to the next. Our main focus will be compositional process, since the autograph shows that most of Bach's entries contain compositional revisions and not merely corrections of copying errors. (In most instances, the autograph preserves a clearly visible initial reading that was partially erased or altered in some way.) On the whole, then, the autograph of the Great Eighteen exemplifies what Robert Marshall has termed a "revision copy," wherein the composer is copying from an existing source but simultaneously making compositional changes more "grammatical" than formative in nature.[16]

In most cases, Bach first entered a reading from the early version. But he also on occasion added material not found in the early version that itself preserves compositional changes. We will limit ourselves to revisions of particular musical interest, and once a certain type of revision has been covered (for example, the alteration of "straight" rhythms to dotted ones), the other occurrences of that type will not necessarily be discussed in any detail. This means that as our coverage proceeds, it will become more general. Nonetheless, it will touch on about every kind of discrepancy that exists between the different versions of these works.

We are admittedly ignorant about some basic issues, for example, the amount of time that elapsed between entries, whether hours, days, weeks, months, or years. Nor can it be ascertained when Bach made the compositional revisions—whether immediately after entering his initial readings or much later—or whether he revised the works one at a time or as a group. But we can be sure that his "master copies" or exemplars were the lost autographs of the early versions of the Great Eighteen (plus the surviving autograph of the early version of the "Nun komm" trio). As he worked, most of his revision must have been purely mental. For despite the numerous discrepancies between versions, only in isolated cases does the autograph itself present much evidence of revision. Given Bach's reputation as a "clean" composer, this comes as no surprise. Still, the possibility exists that in some instances even he might have sketched out revisions beforehand, especially in the case of added material. He certainly relied on sketches elsewhere.

As a point of reference, Table 2-2 enumerates all the compositional revisions in the autograph wherein the original readings are reasonably clear. Such a list has never before been attempted, not even in the critical commentary to Hans Klotz's edition of the Great Eighteen for the *Neue Bach-Ausgabe*, published in the late 1950s. Like so many others before and since, Klotz unhesitatingly accepted the autograph as a *Reinschrift* or "fair copy."[17]

The manuscript contains no title. Perhaps one was intended for the first page, which is entirely blank. In the left upper corner of the first work entered, the Fantasia on "Komm, Heiliger Geist," is the inscription "J. J." (see Figure 2-4). These two letters stand for *Jesu juva* ("Jesus, help"), a motto that Bach frequently penned into his music manuscripts. As he begins, the composer asks for divine guidance. The work heading that follows, which is representative of the manuscript in general, indicates the type of setting (which to Bach, at least, was a "fantasy"), the name of the chorale set, the location of the chorale tune, and the composer: *Fantasia sup[er] Kom heiliger Geist. canto fermo in Pedal. di JS Bach* ("Fantasy on Come Holy Ghost. cantus firmus in the pedal. by J. S. Bach"). To the left of the first stave brace is the inscription *In Organo pleno* ("for full organ"). As was customary, the pedal line appears at the bottom of the left-hand staff, prefaced by the cue *Pedal*.[18]

Thanks to a popular facsimile edition, this page is a familiar sight, and like the manuscript as a whole, it is a masterpiece of calligraphy.[19] Were it not for the use of soprano clef for the right-hand staff, a stan-

TABLE 2-2 Compositional Revisions in the Autograph of the Great Eighteen Chorales

Measure	Beat	Voice	Revision
"Komm, Heiliger Geist, Herre Gott," BWV 651			
53	3–4	alto	♩ changed to ♪ ♫
91	3–4	tenor	note originally faster rhythm than ♩
97	1–2	soprano	note originally faster rhythm than ♩
98	1	tenor	first note changed from a to g
101	1–2	alto 1	note originally faster rhythm than ♩
102	3–4	alto	note originally faster rhythm than ♩
103	1–2	soprano	note originally faster rhythm than ♩
103	3	soprano	second note changed from b′ to a′
"Komm, Heiliger Geist, Herre Gott," BWV 652			
118	2	alto	on second half of beat, eighth note on g′ changed to two sixteenths on g′ and f′
128	2	tenor	on second half of beat, eighth note on e′ changed to two sixteenths on c′-sharp and b
"An Wasserflüssen Babylon," BWV 653			
1	2	alto	rhythm changed from ♫ to ♪♪
2	1–2	alto	original reading is quarter note on g′ followed by eighth note on f′
8	2	bass	pitch changed from A to e
39	2–3	soprano	original reading is half note on a′
79	1–2	soprano	original reading is half note on e″
"Schmücke dich, o liebe Seele," BWV 654			
80	3	soprano	rhythm changed from ♩♩ to ♩. ♪
86	1	soprano	rhythm changed from ♩♩ to ♩. ♪
105	1–2	bass	♩ changed to ♪ 𝄾
"Herr Jesu Christ, dich zu uns wend," BWV 655			
72	2	bass	original reading is eighth note on g followed by eighth rest
"O Lamm Gottes, unschuldig," BWV 656			
55	2	alto	both pitches (a′ and e′) originally half notes
61	1	soprano	original reading is half note on a′
70	2	alto	upper note (a′) originally half note
128	9	alto	pitch changed from f′ to g′

40

Measure	Beat	Voice	Revision

"Von Gott will ich nicht lassen," BWV 658

Measure	Beat	Voice	Revision
7	3	soprano	original reading is four sixteenth notes on d″, b′, g′, and b′

"Nun komm, der Heiden Heiland," BWV 659

Measure	Beat	Voice	Revision
5	2	soprano	original reading lacks appoggiatura on a′
16	3–4	soprano	♩ changed to ♩
24	3–4	soprano	♩ changed to ♩

"Nun komm, der Heiden Heiland," BWV 660

Measure	Beat	Voice	Revision
25	3–4	left-hand	original reading is half note on g

"Allein Gott in der Höh sei Ehr," BWV 663

Measure	Beat	Voice	Revision
26	1	alto	original reading is half note on g′
26	3	alto	original reading is half note on b
27	1	alto	original reading is half note on e′

"Jesus Christus, unser Heiland," BWV 665

Measure	Beat	Voice	Revision
16	2	bass	second note changed from B to c-sharp
29	1–2	soprano	♩ changed to ♩𝄾

dard feature of this source, a modern performer could play from this page almost as easily as from a printed edition. As was his wont, Bach even furnishes directs at the ends of systems to alert the player as to the pitches that begin the next system. Only in the first bar of the bottom system, where the last note of the tenor voice intersects the beam used for the alto's sixteenth notes, is there some uncertainty about pitch or rhythm. Here, to alleviate any potential confusion, the tablature symbol for f-sharp indicates the correct pitch.

Of course, it was easy for Bach to produce a note-perfect page in this instance because he was merely copying the first twenty-seven measures of the early version. The two versions agree completely until measure 43, at which point the composer decided to set all ten phrases of this unusually long chorale melody, rather than, as in the early version, just phrases 1, 2, 3, and 8. In so doing, he increased the work's size from 48 to 106 bars, by far the most dramatic instance of sectional expansion in any of the Great Eighteen chorales.

In addition to being about twice as long as a normal chorale, this tune is extraordinarily repetitive: phrases 2 and 6 are identical, as are 3 and 7; phrases 4 and 8 are the same except at the end; and phrases

FIGURE 2-4. Autograph score of "Komm, Heiliger Geist, Herre Gott," BWV 651, mm. 1–27 (Staatsbibliothek zu Berlin—Preussischer Kulturbesitz, Musikabteilung mit Mendelssohn-Archiv, Mus. ms. Bach P 271, p. 58)

1 and 5 conclude with the same stepwise ascent. This large amount of shared material is the reason that phrases 2–4 and 6–8 are set to virtually the same music (mm. 55–86 are a note-for-note repeat of mm. 12–43). Bach had to compose new music only for the end of phrase 4 and the first three measures of phrase 5, along with an interlude between the two phrases. Not surprisingly, this newly composed passage, found at measures 44–54, preserves the first compositional revision (see Figure 2-5). It occurs in the third measure of the penultimate system of the second page (m. 53), where the large size of the alto's b-natural quarter note on beat 3 shows that the original reading was a half note. The musical effect of the change—always the most important question—is greater rhythmic activity between the inner voices.

All the remaining compositional revisions take place in the other newly composed section, measures 89–103, which contains the ninth and tenth phrases of the chorale tune. (The "coda" that follows in mm. 104–6 comes note-for-note from the conclusion of the early version.) The intense compositional activity here is due simply to the use of new thematic material: to set the word "Hallelujah," Bach introduces in measure 89 a fugue subject that he will manipulate for a full fifteen bars. In the newly composed passage at measures 44–54, he sticks with the same accompanimental theme stated at the outset.

The second newly composed section confines itself, conveniently, to the last page of this entry, shown in Figure 2-6. Just as soon as the new theme appears for the first time, in the last bar of the top system, alto voice, Bach's script begins to lose its beautiful, calligraphic appearance, especially with regard to the placement of accidentals and spacing between notes. To focus on the compositional revisions, the one in measure 98, which changed that inverted statement of the fugue subject from real to tonal, was dictated by the prevailing G-minor harmony. In five other instances, a half note was fashioned from some faster rhythm, but exactly which is impossible to say since all values less than a half note have the same size of note head (and same length of stem). Still, in all these revisions save that in measure 102, the half note is preceded by the first seven sixteenth notes of the subject, in the same voice, implying eighths or sixteenths. An eighth note would have continued the theme, while a sixteenth would have allowed for back-to-back statements of its first half, as in measures 90, 93–96, and 100.

Bach might well have made some additional revisions here, for his exposition of the "Hallelujah" theme is marred by minor inconsistencies, such as one might expect from a composing score. Only the tenor statement in measures 92–93 ends like the first one, with a trill followed by two thirty-second notes. For no apparent musical reason, the

FIGURE 2-5. Autograph score of "Komm, Heiliger Geist, Herre Gott," BWV 651, mm. 28–57 (Staatsbibliothek zu Berlin—Preussischer Kulturbesitz, Musikabteilung mit Mendelssohn-Archiv, Mus. ms. Bach P 271, p. 59)

FIGURE 2-6. Autograph score of "Komm, Heiliger Geist, Herre Gott," BWV 651, mm. 86–106 (Staatsbibliothek zu Berlin—Preussischer Kulturbesitz, Musik-abteilung mit Mendelssohn-Archiv, Mus. ms. Bach P 271, p. 61)

45

second and third statements conclude with an anticipatory sixteenth note instead, and the final statement lacks a trill symbol. The performer should have no compunction about playing all three statements just like the initial one, with a trill followed by two ascending thirty-seconds.

On the next page of the manuscript appears a second setting of the same chorale, marked *alio modo* ("a different way"), a designation likewise used by Bach for chorales with multiple settings in the *Orgelbüchlein* and Part III of the *Clavierübung*. (As Figure 2-2 attests, Altnikol also used this formulation.) Due to the lengthening of the cadences of phrases 2–4 and 6–8, the revised version here is also longer than the early version, but only by six bars.

Example 2-1, taken from Heinz Lohmann's edition, illustrates the reworking of the first of these cadences (mm. 39–42), with the readings from the early version appearing in small print at the top of the system.[20] This passage was expanded by one measure at the beginning, while the last two bars were kept more or less intact. Here the revised version improves on the early one through its use of contrary motion and suspensions between the inner voices, its tasteful introduction of sixteenth notes, and its relatively active pedal line.

The tendency to lengthen and embellish is central to Bach's revisional practice. Almost without exception, whenever he changed the length of a work when reworking it he made it longer, and he almost never simplified material during the process. How, then, is one to account for the higher degree of ornamentation throughout the soprano voice of the early version? The only plausible explanation is that this ornamentation stems not from Bach but, at some point in the manuscript transmission, from a copyist (which would by no means be an unusual circumstance in the Bach sources). Not only does the ornamentation pose an exception to what we know about Bach's techniques of revision; it is also distinctly un-Bachian in its simultaneous use of ornamented (upward stems) and unornamented readings (downward stems). One Bach-circle copyist fond of this quirky notation is J. G. Walther, and both sources for the early version—one of which is by Walther's pupil J. T. Krebs—could very well stem from a lost Walther copy.[21]

As for the two compositional revisions in this entry, in both instances Bach copied from the early version an eighth note but, to intensify the rhythm, changed the reading to two sixteenths. These changes are completely analogous to the differences between the versions in measure 51, but there the autograph itself preserves no evidence of revision.

The next entry in the manuscript, titled "An Waßer Flüßen Babylon a 2 Clav. et Pedal di J. S. Bach," is also six measures longer than its early version, thanks to an ingenious extension of the final cadence. As

EXAMPLE 2-1. "Komm, Heiliger Geist, Herre Gott," BWV 652/652a, as edited
by Heinz Lohmann, Edition Breitkopf 6587. Breitkopf & Härtel, Wiesbaden—
Leipzig. Used by permission.

in the first setting of "Komm, Heiliger Geist," one of the compositional
revisions (that in m. 79) takes place in this newly composed section.
Three compositional changes are preserved here in the first eight measures alone (see Figure 2-7), and in each case the original reading apparently stems from the early version (BWV 653a).[22]

In the opening measure, as indicated by the high placement of the
dot and the close spacing between the first two notes, the alto originally
contained on beat 2 the relatively prosaic reading of an eighth note and
two sixteenths. The soprano rhythm on the next beat was likewise sharp-

FIGURE 2-7. Autograph score of "Komm, Heiliger Geist, Herre Gott," BWV 652, mm. 191–99; and "An Wasserflüssen Babylon," BWV 653, mm. 1–29 (Staatsbibliothek zu Berlin—Preussischer Kulturbesitz, Musikabteilung mit Mendelssohn-Archiv, Mus. ms. Bach P 271, p. 66)

ened to a dotted eighth and two thirty-seconds, but there only the revised reading was ever notated.

On the first beat of measure 2, the misshapen note head of the last alto note shows that the pitch was originally f′, and the first two notes are too close together for an eighth followed by a sixteenth. The deformed note head is just far enough away from the first note to have begun a new beat. Thus, the original reading was evidently that found in the early version, a quarter note on g′ followed by an eighth note on f′ (or at least a note head for the latter). Bach surely aimed this revision at the stasis that results from yet another alto quarter note.

His alteration in measure 8, conversely, achieves harmonic variety. Here an erasure shows that the original pitch was lower, and it must have been A, as in the early version. This revision adds an E-minor chord to a measure whose only harmony in the early version is G major (the A serves only as a passing tone). Although the same discrepancy exists between the two versions on the repeat of this passage (m. 20), the revision there is purely mental.

Any reference here to the "early version" of this piece means the version known as BWV 653a, the model for the revised version entered by Bach into the autograph of the Great Eighteen. But a third version of this composition (which also lacks the six-bar coda) exists as well, a five-part setting with double pedal and with the ornamental chorale tune in the soprano. Known as BWV 653b, it is taken by most scholars today as the original version of this work complex.[23]

Such a view is understandable, since the figuration of both the accompaniment and the solo chorale tune is less ornate than in the other two versions. Still, in light of Bach's strong tendency to embellish as he revised, it is hard to believe he would have simplified the texture from five to four voices. Are there *any* documented cases in which he resorted to textural simplification? Furthermore, as Robert Marshall has recently argued, Bach's authorship of the double-pedal version seems highly dubious on its own terms, for the double pedal "tends to obscure and complicate rather than to enrich the texture."[24] To cite perhaps the most egregious examples, the subdominant inflections in measure 14 and especially in measures 73–75 sound downright crude (see Example 2-2). Could Bach have devised such primitive harmonies— none of which appear in either of the other two versions—as late as his Weimar period?

The evidence either way is inconclusive, but it is entirely possible that the double-pedal version was arranged from BWV 653a by someone other than Bach. Again, the prime candidate is Walther, who prepared copies of both BWV 653a and 653b. One thing is for sure: the

EXAMPLE 2-2. "An Wasserflüssen Babylon," BWV 653b

double-pedal version had absolutely no impact on the final version. Despite its popularity among organists, BWV 653b plays only a marginal role in the collection known as the Great Eighteen chorales.[25]

To return to Bach's compilation of the Great Eighteen, he next entered "Schmücke dich." Compared to the previous work, in which only sixteen of the eighty-three bars of the revised version remain unchanged from the early one, the revision here is slight. Both versions are the same length, and the alterations are mostly directed at the honing of certain rhythms. The latter is true, for example, of the first two compositional revisions in the autograph entry, where in both instances a pair of eighth notes from the early version was altered to a dotted eighth and sixteenth. In measure 86, this change heightens the very real sense that measures 85–92 are a varied repeat of measures 76–83, since at the analogous spot in the earlier passage Bach let the eighth notes stand.

A revision of a different sort occurs in measure 105. In the early version, a pedal point on F extends from the beginning of this bar until the downbeat of measure 107. Probably because this pedal point merely doubled the sustained f′ in the soprano, it was replaced with wide-ranging motivic figuration. Bach copied from the early version the half note that begins the measure but—bearing in mind that the time signature is $\frac{3}{4}$—changed his mind before drawing the dot.

He next notated the trio on "Herr Jesu Christ." Both versions of this chorale are also the same length. Although several discrepant readings exist between the two, the most interesting of which involve the contour of the ritornello theme,[26] this entry preserves only one compositional revision. It takes place one measure from the end (m. 72), where the penultimate statement of the main pedal motive (♩♪♩♩♪♩♪) was rewritten to end on a quarter note rather than an eighth.

To understand the context of the revision, consider that measures 1–51 of this work constitute a free ritornello form in which the pedal motive appears ten times, that measures 52–69 largely abandon the ritornello and completely forsake the pedal motive in favor of a phrase-by-phrase rendering of the chorale tune in the pedals, and that measures 70–73 form a coda in which the ritornello is reinstated and accompanied by two further statements of the pedal motive. The only other statement of the pedal motive in either version that ends with a quarter note—Bach's way of fortifying the final cadence—is the very last one (mm. 72–73). Since these last two statements comprise a back-to-back unit effectively isolated from all other statements, it makes sense that they have the same rhythm.

The next entry, the three-verse setting of "O Lamm Gottes," is of special interest. For one thing, Bach recast over 30 of the 120 bars of the early version, especially in Variation 2. He also switched the time signature of the third variation from $\frac{9}{8}$ to $\frac{9}{4}$ (and, beginning in m. 135 of the revised version, to $\frac{3}{2}$) and, consequently, replaced all eighth-note triplets with quarters. This change may be thought of as a correction dictated by the half-note pulse of the pedal line.[27] A further difference is that the early version is six bars shorter, as the repeat in Variation 2 lacks measures 64–69. This omission results in an alarmingly swift move to the next phrase of the chorale melody.

Three of the four compositional revisions in the autograph entry occur in the second variation as well. Those in measures 55 and 70 entail the arpeggiation of an A-major triad in the so-called *style brisé* (broken style). In the early version, however, the arpeggiation in both passages is temporarily impeded by a half note on e'. Bach eliminated this defect by using quarter notes instead, not only for this voice but for the upper alto voice as well.

As for the revision in measure 61, once again a half note was changed to a quarter. But in another respect, this is a truly exceptional, even unique, occurrence in this manuscript: it is the only instance of a revised passage, as opposed to one newly composed, whose original reading can be identified as something other than that found in the early version (which has four sixteenths on this beat). Bach did not rely on the early version here, obviously, because its soprano voice is an octave higher at this juncture (and for most of the previous bar as well). The result would have been a jarring upward leap of a ninth.

His next entry, "Nun danket alle Gott," is another matter entirely, since this is the work least changed from its early version. The amount of revision here is so negligible, in fact, that no edition of the early version exists (not even in the *Neue Bach-Ausgabe*) and no listing for it is to be found in the *Bach-Werke-Verzeichnis*. As is true of all the remaining entries except the second setting of "Allein Gott," both versions are the same length.

The only difference between the two is the length of the soprano note that ends the *Stollen*, which in the early version is notated as two tied whole notes. Bach's concern here, presumably, was how this note extended through the modulation to the dominant that occurs in the second ending. For once the music starts to change keys, this note loses its sense of finality. Cutting it off in the middle of the measure neatly avoided this problem. Although no modulation occurs in the first ending, the note was shortened there as well, for the sake of uniformity.

Bach next notated "Von Gott will ich nicht lassen." He added many fast rhythms to the accompaniment, as well as passing tones to the chorale tune. Yet the autograph preserves only one compositional revision, illustrating the former type of alteration.

The first setting of "Nun komm" follows. Here the ornamental chorale tune was embellished in various places and certain rhythms were sharpened as well, allowing for a better musical flow. The revisions in measures 16 and 24 both involve the lengthening of a cadential tone in this line from a quarter to a half note, in accordance with the cadence in measure 8.

Bach next entered a second setting of this hymn. In addition to changing the time signature (for whatever reasons) from cut time to common time, he revised the ornamental chorale tune here in much the same way as in the previous work. But in measures 25–26 he also improved the contour of the part, even to the extent of transposing two sixteenth notes (on f-sharp and g′) up an octave. As the one compositional revision evinces, he embellished the left-hand voice as well.

A third setting of this chorale follows. Its autograph entry contains no compositional revisions. Still, numerous discrepant readings exist between the two versions, most notably those that affect how the fugal countersubject ends. For reasons that remain unclear, Bach also rebarred this work from common time with sixteenths as the basic subdivision to cut time with eighth notes. As a result, the revised version has twice as many measures—but the amount of material is identical.

Nor is there any evidence of compositional activity in the next entry, the first of three settings of "Allein Gott." Bach did, however, make some minor improvements to the early version, most of which involve the ornamental chorale tune. For example, the strikingly beautiful sixteenth-note triplets in measure 14 were originally a pair of anapests.

As for the second setting of this hymn, its two versions differ substantially, especially with regard to rhythmic sharpening of the ornamental chorale tune and refinement of accompanimental figuration. The latter is represented by the three compositional revisions in the autograph entry, in which the original readings are rather more homophonic. Most interesting is the expansion of the cadenza-like passage in measure 96 from one to two bars, which makes the revised version one measure longer.

After this entry, lest we forget, Bach laid aside the autograph for about four years' time. When he returned to it, it was to notate a third setting of "Allein Gott," the magisterial trio setting in A major. The revised version here almost amounts to a systematic reworking of all three voices with respect to contour, rhythm, and ornamentation.[28] These differences notwithstanding, no compositional revisions are apparent in the autograph.

The last of the Great Eighteen chorales entered by Bach himself is the first setting of "Jesus Christus, unser Heiland." Among the several changes made to the early version is the addition of chromatic notes (all of them c-sharps) above the final pedal point. Of the two compositional revisions in the autograph, that in measure 16 allowed the bass voice to sound consecutively all seven degrees of the E-minor scale, instead of leaping from the fifth to the seventh. The same discrepancy exists between the two versions in measures 18–19, where this material appears in the dominant key, but there only the reading with the complete scale was entered.

An important realization to be drawn from this survey is that Bach's first three entries into this manuscript are the only ones with a significant amount of added material. One might also say, therefore, that these three entries are the most revised. This statement suggests that when he began to compile the Great Eighteen, Bach's energy was particularly high. Could it be that later on in the process his enthusiasm waned? This would explain not only the four-year hiatus between the thirteenth and fourteenth settings but also—as we will discuss in the next chapter—the likelihood that the collection was never properly completed.

It is infinitely more important, though, to realize that in no instance was Bach content just to copy a work: some inner force drove him as well to revise every one of the fifteen chorales he entered. This force, which may be regarded as the basic and final objective of the composer's methodology, was nothing less than the quest for perfection.[29] Accordingly, the revised versions of the Great Eighteen chorales do not represent the "definitive" or "final" forms of these masterworks. They merely advance the music toward its ultimate goal.

Chapter 3

SIGNIFICANCE

Whatever the word "significance" might imply, it seems fitting for a chapter on function, purpose, and structure. To be more specific, our discussion here will tackle such issues as the liturgical and organological context of the music, the role it played in Bach's evolution as a composer, and Bach's criteria for ordering the works as he did when he brought them together as a collection.

Not all these themes are new. For example, we established in chapter 1 that the Great Eighteen served as a catalyst for Bach's assimilation of the Italian concerto style. Throughout the collection, he superimposes this foreign idiom onto the chorale types cultivated by his forebears; he "sanctifies" the concerto form. Since it gave unprecedented importance to the accompanimental voices, this fusion of styles expanded these chorale types to unheard-of proportions. It also led to hybrid designs of great sumptuousness and intricacy. To quote Manfred Bukofzer, the Great Eighteen "transcend by their magnitude and depth all previous types of chorale prelude."[1] To be sure, the sheer size of the individual works is one of their most salient traits, and one greatly admired by commentators over the years.

Enter Albert Schweitzer. In his highly influential Bach monograph, originally published in 1905, Schweitzer, too, hailed the Great Eighteen as "masterpieces."[2] Yet in a remarkable aside instigated by the *pedaliter* setting of "Jesus Christus, unser Heiland" from Part III of the *Clavierübung*, he also revealed an intense dislike of "long" chorale arrangements. Schweitzer faulted this work for its fragmented chorale melody, which results from the use of a long ritornello between all

phrases. His criticism applies just as well to the Great Eighteen chorales, many of which, as we saw in chapter 1, adopt this same procedure. He concluded that once the accompanimental voices of a chorale
setting "become an independent picture, in which the lines of the *cantus firmus* follow one another at long intervals, we get a piece of music
that is neither intellectually nor formally satisfactory."

What Schweitzer is really saying is that the ideal chorale setting is
one that presents the chorale melody in continuous fashion; in such a
work, the accompanimental voices are perforce always subordinate. Not
surprisingly, the Bach organ chorales especially championed by the
great humanitarian are those that closely follow this prototype: the chorales of the *Orgelbüchlein*.

If the job of the chorale arranger is merely to render the melody as
sung by a congregation, perhaps Schweitzer has a point. But a more reasonable attitude is that other designs are equally viable. With regard to
the Great Eighteen, is it not the independent structure posed by the accompanimental figuration—the very feature disdained by Schweitzer—
that so attracts us to the music? Who has not marveled at the composer's ability in these works to present simultaneously the hymn tune
and a second, equally compelling form in the accompaniment?

As a composer of organ chorales, Bach could be quite intimate, as
in the *Orgelbüchlein*, or he could aim for something a bit more epic in
its outlook. In either realm, his mastery is unparalleled. And so, rather
than alleging that the Great Eighteen are fundamentally defective due
to their complex structure, it seems more sensible to appreciate them
on their own terms. Those terms, in the emphatic words of Harvey Grace,
include a "workmanship as nearly flawless as we have a right to expect
from a mere human."[3]

FUNCTION AND PURPOSE

Bach composed most of the Great Eighteen, like the majority of his
organ works, while he was organist at the Weimar court. According to
the nineteenth-century Bach biographer Philipp Spitta, these chorale
settings represent "the very quintessence of all he elaborated in Weimar
in this field of art."[4]

The ruler of the court, Duke Wilhelm Ernst, was, true to his sur-
name, a serious-minded man.[5] The duke was childless and separated
from his wife, and religion was his passion. He demanded that all his
subjects regularly attend services at the court chapel, as he faithfully
did himself, and he even quizzed them on the sermons preached there.

Someone who took such an interest in theological matters must also have had strong feelings about liturgical music. Luckily for Bach, the duke looked with favor on his chapel organist. According to Bach's obituary, "The pleasure His Grace took in his playing fired him with the desire to try every possible artistry in his treatment of the organ."[6] The awesome diversity of the Great Eighteen chorales bears eloquent witness to this statement.

Despite some Pietist leanings, Wilhelm subscribed to the orthodox Lutheran faith (as, of course, did his organist). Surely, then, the duke appreciated Bach's predilection for chorales from the Reformation period. Four of the hymns set among the early versions of the Great Eighteen are by Luther himself, and five others are from 1522–63. The remaining three are from no later than the middle of the seventeenth century.

To judge from Lutheran practice, Bach regularly played for a variety of worship services: the *Hauptgottesdienst* held on the mornings of the Sundays and festivals of the church year, the vigil services prior to the festivals, the *Vespergottesdienst* that took place on Sunday afternoon, and daily prayer and preaching services. He would also have played for weddings and funerals. These different services required different types of chorales. For example, the chorales normally used for the *Hauptgottesdienst* were *de tempore*, designated for a specific time in the liturgical year. Those used for the *Vespergottesdienst* were *omne tempore*, suitable at any time of the year.

Our best source for Bach's understanding of hymnody during his Weimar period (and in general) is the autograph of the *Orgelbüchlein*.[7] Significantly, this source lists in liturgical order ten of the twelve chorales set among the early versions of the Great Eighteen. Included in the *de tempore* section of this manuscript are "Nun komm" (Advent), "O Lamm Gottes" (Passiontide), "Komm, Heiliger Geist" (Pentecost), "Komm, Gott Schöpfer" (Pentecost), "Herr Jesu Christ" (Pentecost), and "Allein Gott" (Trinity). The *omne tempore* portion contains "An Wasserflüssen Babylon" ("Christian Life and Conduct"), "Von Gott will ich nicht lassen" ("Christian Life and Conduct"), "Wenn wir in höchsten Nöten sein" ("Christian Life and Conduct"), and "Jesus Christus, unser Heiland" ("The Lord's Supper"). "Schmücke dich" appears in an appendix that contains hymns for miscellaneous needs and occasions. It has traditionally been regarded as an *omne tempore* chorale, especially appropriate at communion.

Bach may not have, in every instance, strictly adhered to this classification. For one thing, the Weimar court chapel may have followed the widespread practice of singing "Herr Jesu Christ" and "Allein Gott" during the *Hauptgottesdienst* on most Sundays of the year.[8] Whatever

the case, it stands to reason that "Herr Jesu Christ" was a particular
favorite in Weimar, as Wilhelm's grandfather, Wilhelm II of Weimar, is
said to have authored its first three stanzas.

As to how Bach incorporated the Great Eighteen chorales into the
Weimar liturgy, consider again their large size. In performance, they
range from about two and a half minutes ("Komm, Gott Schöpfer") all
the way to nine (the ornamental "Komm, Heiliger Geist"); their aver-
age length is around five minutes. Hence, in contrast to the miniature
settings of the *Orgelbüchlein*, they would have been much too long for
preludes to or as interludes between the stanzas of regular congregational hymns. As such, they would have greatly diminished the all-im-
portant role of congregational singing in the Lutheran service.

But as Robin Leaver has recently discussed, the Great Eighteen
would have served ideally as preludes to communion hymns, for these
required an extended introduction to cover the distribution of the ele-
ments, particularly on major festivals.[9] Leaver also points out that many
of the hymns set in the collection have strong eucharistic connections.
For instance, "O Lamm Gottes" is a paraphrase of the Agnus Dei, which
belongs to the communion rite of the Lutheran liturgy. Similarly, "An
Wasserflüssen Babylon" was the standard tune for Paul Gerhardt's
hymn "Ein Lämmlein geht und trägt die Schuld," which has close ties
to the Agnus Dei as well. "Schmücke dich" and "Jesus Christus, unser
Heiland" are classic communion hymns. Indeed, Bach's autograph
entry of the *pedaliter* "Jesus Christus" contains the indication *sub Comunione*. One may assume, then, that Bach utilized the works in precisely this way.

The chapel's organ was constructed in 1658 by Ludwig Compenius
and rebuilt in 1707–8 by J. Conrad Weishaupt and in 1713–14 by
Heinrich Nicolaus Trebs. Although the instrument no longer survives,
we have a good idea about its specifications, at least as of 1737, when
its stop list was first published (see Figure 3-1).[10] Whoever remarked
that Bach never had at his disposal an organ equal to his talent might
well have been thinking of this modest, two-manual instrument. Its design typifies Thuringian organ building in the early 1700s, especially
with regard to the three string stops (manual Gemsshorn 8′ and Viol di
Gamba 8′ and pedal Violon-Bass 16′) and the predominance of stops
in general at eight-foot pitch or lower.[11] The pedal Posaun-Bass 16′ and
Glockenspiel are also specifically Thuringian.

Considering the huge influence of the Italian string repertoire on the
Great Eighteen, these string stops seem a perfect complement to the
music. For example, as the organ historian Barbara Owen has observed,

Ober Clavier, CD-c'''	Unter Clavier, CD-c'''	Pedal, C-e'
1. Principal 8', tin*	1. Principal 8', tin	1. Gross Untersatz 32', wood
2. Quintadena 16', metal*	2. Viol di Gamba 8', metal	2. Sub-Bass 16', wood
3. Gemsshorn 8', metal*	3. Gedackt 8', metal*	3. Posaun-Bass 16', wood*
4. Grobgedackt 8' metal	4. Trompete 8', metal*	4. Violon-Bass 16', wood
5. Quintadena 4', metal	5. klein Gedackt 4', metal	5. Principal-Bass 8', metal
6. Octava 4', metal	6. Octava 4', metal	6. Trompeta-Bass 8', metal
7. Mixtur 6 ranks, metal	7. Wald-Flöthe 2', metal*	7. Cornett-Bass 4', metal
8. Cymbel 3 ranks, metal*	8. Sesquialtera 4 ranks "in Octava, aus 3 und 2 Fuss"	
9. A Glockenspiel "und Spiel-Register dazu" ("with stop knob")		

Accessories

Tremulant for the Hauptwerk

Tremulant for the Unterwerk

Oberwerk to Pedal coupler

Manual coupler

Cymbel Stern

*From the Compenius organ of 1658.

FIGURE 3-1 Specifications of the Compenius-Weishaupt-Trebs organ in the Weimar court chapel, as described in 1737

"The walking bass in the first setting of *Nun komm, der Heiden Heiland* cries out for a distinct-sounding Violone."[12] Bach might even have played the two free trios with nothing but these stops, using the Gemsshorn 8' on the *Ober Clavier*, the Viol di Gamba 8' on the *Unter Clavier*, and the Violon-Bass 16' on the *Pedal*.

The instrument's tuning probably benefited from the growing trend in the early eighteenth century toward equal temperament, especially considering that Andreas Werckmeister, the leading advocate of well-tempered tuning at the time, exerted a strong influence on both of Weimar's principal organists: Bach obviously relied on Werckmeister's *Orgelprobe* in testing organs,[13] and the organist of the Weimar town church, J. G. Walther, was one of Werckmeister's pupils. In any event, the Great Eighteen settings of "Schmücke dich" and "Von Gott will ich nicht lassen," in the keys of E-flat major and F minor, are seriously at odds with the old mean-tone tunings of the seventeenth century.

A visitor to Weimar today will find no trace of the chapel, for it burned to the ground about twenty-five years after Bach's death. Known as the Himmelsburg or "Castle of heaven," this edifice was the very picture of grandeur. Its three stories were splendiferously decorated, and its focal point was a three-layer structure that consisted of (from ground level up) an altar, pulpit, and giant obelisk. Most remarkable, directly above this complex, within a cupola-shaped, balustraded gallery, stood the organ. Both gallery and organ are plainly visible in the famous gouache by Christian Richter, circa 1660, shown in Figure 3-2.[14] Such magnificence no doubt enhanced the act of worship for Wilhelm and his entourage. But given the stratospheric placement of the organ (about sixty feet off the ground) and the narrow opening in the ceiling (roughly nine by twelve feet) through which the instrument's sounds filtered down into the room, did the congregation fully comprehend the aforementioned "artistry" of its organist?

Regardless of the answer, we can say with confidence that the Great Eighteen originated out of Bach's need for liturgical organ music. Decades later, around 1740, when Bach began to assemble the pieces into a collection, he obviously thought of them differently. In Leipzig, he was under no obligation to compose or perform organ music. Furthermore, although he continued to write for and play the instrument his whole life, it had been over twenty years since he had actually held an organ post.

During this interim, Bach's tendency to collect his works—a pattern begun by the *Orgelbüchlein*—prominently asserts itself. From his years in Cöthen (1717–23) right up to 1740, a steady stream of collections, mostly for keyboard, flowed from his pen. They include (in roughly chronological order) the Sonatas and Partitas for Unaccompanied Violin; the Brandenburg Concertos; Book I of the *Well-Tempered Clavier*; the Inventions and Sinfonias; the French and English Suites; the Suites for Unaccompanied Cello; the Six Harpsichord Partitas; Parts II–III of the *Clavierübung*; the eight concertos for harpsichord and orchestra, BWV 1052–59; and possibly Book II of the *Well-Tempered Clavier*, which dates from either the late 1730s or the early 1740s. (One might also cite the series of "chorale cantatas" from 1724–25 that form the

FIGURE 3-2. Interior of the Weimar court chapel, painting by Christian Richter, ca. 1660 (*Kunstsammlungen zu Weimar*)

second annual cycle of Bach's Leipzig church cantatas.) The list continues in the 1740s with such collections as the Goldberg Variations; the *Art of Fugue*; the Musical Offering; the Canonic Variations on "Vom Himmel hoch"; the fourteen Goldberg canons, BWV 1087; and the "Schübler" chorales.

Printed collectively in 1731 as Part I of the *Clavierübung* (literally, "keyboard exercise"), the Six Harpsichord Partitas commenced the most extensive publishing venture of Bach's life. Part II of the series, containing the Italian Concerto and French Overture, appeared in 1735; Part III, a set of twenty-one organ chorales and six free works, followed in 1739; and Part IV, the Goldberg Variations, followed in 1741.[15] As a further keyboard collection begun in the late 1730s or early 1740s, the Great Eighteen have much in common with the *Clavierübung*, and scholars have long speculated that Bach compiled them as well with an eye to publication. This theory becomes more plausible still when we realize that chorale settings were virtually the only type of organ music published by the composer during his lifetime (see the organ chorales of Part III of the *Clavierübung*, the Canonic Variations on "Vom Himmel hoch," and the Schübler chorales, published around 1748). Why would he not have desired to share these fruits of his labors with the widest possible audience?

Still, in assembling this collection Bach must also have been motivated by other, more internal factors. One of these was retrospection. As he entered his final decade, he had begun to take stock of his life's work, much as he had taken stock of his genealogy five years earlier by writing a brief history of the Bach family.[16] This trend manifests itself in a number of collections that pulled together, in revised or transcribed form, pieces composed decades earlier: the eight harpsichord concertos (ca. 1738), the Great Eighteen and Book II of the *Well-Tempered Clavier* (ca. 1739–42), and the Schübler chorales (ca. 1748).[17] This pattern culminates with the B-Minor Mass—not a collection per se but a collection of movements from various periods of the composer's life— which was not finalized until a year or so before Bach's death. In collecting and revising these pieces, which he must have counted among his very best, he was preserving his handiwork for posterity.

The Great Eighteen also epitomize various chorale types—the chorale motet, the chorale partita, the ornamental chorale, and the cantus firmus chorale—that reach back to the early seventeenth century. As a collection created around 1740, they look back at these old chorale types from the distance of more than a century. The collection, then, is retrospective in a historical as well as personal sense.

Like so many of Bach's collections, the Great Eighteen are also genre-specific. As such, they constitute a compositional treatise on the organ chorale. They also amount to a method of "advanced" organ playing—to paraphrase Harold Gleason—with chapters on various techniques and styles. Some pieces are essays in gossamer filigree, where either the right or left hand gingerly negotiates a minefield of ornaments. Others, such as the first setting of "Komm, Heiliger Geist" and the third setting of "Nun komm," are manual exercises in perpetual motion. Hardest of all are the trios, where both the hands and feet are extraordinarily busy. No composer had ever written such complex chorale settings or demanded so much from an organist.

This combination of performing and compositional virtuosity is a Bachian trademark, and it is but one way in which the Great Eighteen reflect his music in general. For, as a collection devoted to a single genre, they also reveal the encyclopedic and systematic nature of Bach's approach to composition.[18] As a group of organ works, they symbolize the instrument we most associate with this composer (and the instrument whose repertory he dominates like no other composer dominates any other repertory). As a group of chorale settings, they explore a genre—Luther's vernacular congregational hymn—that Bach knew more intimately than any composer before or after him.[19] Like Bach's music as a whole, the Great Eighteen also represent a culmination of centuries-old forms and styles. In short, they are a true microcosm of Bach's unique art.

THE STRUCTURE OF THE COLLECTION

Having discussed the purpose and function of the music, let us now look at the makeup of the Great Eighteen as a collected entity. We will begin with the question of the precise number of works that properly comprise the set.

At the crux of this matter, of course, is the autograph manuscript. Since this source also includes the Canonic Variations on "Vom Himmel hoch," it actually contains nineteen pieces. But no one has ever been tempted to group this work along with the other eighteen. For one thing, as a set of five independent movements the Canonic Variations are a fundamentally different sort of composition: they form a collection just by themselves. Also in contrast to all the other works in the manuscript, with the possible exception of "Vor deinen Thron," the Canonic Variations seem to have been composed toward the end of Bach's life; there is no evidence of the piece before 1746.[20] Bach may have added it to the autograph of the Great Eighteen simply because that source was at hand. His intent might also have been to form a hand-written anthology of organ chorales.

The work that follows the Canonic Variations in the autograph is "Vor deinen Thron." In his edition for the *Neue Bach-Ausgabe*, Hans Klotz also excluded this piece from the collection because of its physical separation from the first seventeen works in the manuscript and its special status as Bach's "deathbed" chorale.[21] He thus rechristened the set as the Seventeen Chorales (*Siebzehn Choräle*). Assuming that Altnikol's entries were made after Bach's death, the fact that the anonymous copyist placed "Vor deinen Thron" after the Canonic Variations rather than after the *pedaliter* "Jesus Christus, unser Heiland" would seem to support Klotz's decision.

Klotz, however, retained both of Altnikol's entries, the *manualiter* setting of "Jesus Christus, unser Heiland" and "Komm, Gott Schöpfer." Indeed, he never once doubted that Bach instructed Altnikol to copy these two pieces into the manuscript. As we will see later, Klotz even regarded the latter work as a linchpin in the collection's overall structure. But the likelihood that Altnikol entered these works on his own initiative means they belong less to the collection proper than does "Vor deinen Thron."

Given these circumstances, it is imperative to distinguish and prioritize between the fifteen works in Bach's hand and the three that are not. This does not mean, however, that the two groups are mutually exclusive. The former might be thought of as the "real" collection (the Great Fifteen?) drawn up by the composer and the combined contents as a somewhat more loosely organized anthology compiled by members of the Bach circle (neither of these entities, though, displays a truly unified structure). At the very least, one must concede that all eighteen works are united in two important ways: they are all relatively large chorale settings; and all of them, with the possible exception of "Vor deinen Thron," are revised versions of works composed during Bach's Weimar period. (Did Altnikol also choose his entries with these two aspects in mind?) They belong to no other collection, and they share too many commonalities for any of them to be excluded.

Besides, it is as the Great Eighteen or some variation thereof that these pieces have been known for almost two centuries. And it is by this moniker that they continue to be recognized among the vast majority of organists, musicologists, and music lovers on both sides of the Atlantic today. The sense of familiarity imparted by this tradition is somehow quite significant.

The first person to refer to "eighteen" chorales was the antiquarian Georg Poelchau (1773–1836), who owned the autograph in the early nineteenth century. The title page he drew up for the manuscript contains the designation *Achtzehn noch ungedruckte Choralvorspiele* (Eighteen still unpublished chorale preludes).[22]

Some years later, we find the first reference to these works as "great." It appears in their first collected edition, that by Felix Mendelssohn published in 1846 under the titles *15 Grand Preludes on Corales* and *15 Grosse Choral-Vorspiele für die Orgel*. Mendelssohn's use of this adjective here is clearly in contradistinction to the "small" settings of the *Orgelbüchlein*, which he had edited the previous year under the title *44 kleine Choralvorspiele*.

A year later, all the pieces were published in piecemeal fashion in volumes 6 and 7 of the Peters edition of Bach's complete organ works, edited by Friedrich Conrad Griepenkerl and Ferdinand Roitzsch. These tomes also contain all the chorales from Part III of the *Clavierübung* and a number of miscellaneous large settings as well. The collective title of the two volumes is—once again, expressly in contrast to the *Orgelbüchlein*—*Grössere und kunstreichere Choralvorspiele* (Larger and more artistic chorale preludes). In his text-critical remarks, Griepenkerl also speaks of "eighteen chorale preludes."

In his edition for the Bachgesellschaft of 1878, Wilhelm Rust opted for the title, in imitation of the Schübler chorales, *Achtzehn Choräle von verschiedener art* (Eighteen chorales of various kinds). But his preface also refers to the collection as *Achtzehn Choräle, die sogenannten grossen* (Eighteen chorales, the so-called great). Thus, by the late nineteenth century, Mendelssohn's designation had gained considerable currency.

It remained only for "great" and "eighteen" to be mentioned in the same breath. When this became common practice is impossible to determine, but by 1937 E. Power Biggs was citing the collection as the "Eighteen Great."[23] If the secondary literature is any indication, the accepted usage by the 1950s in the United States had become the "Great Eighteen." British and German commentators throughout the twentieth century, though, have tended to avoid the adjective altogether. The Eighteen is still the nickname of choice in the United Kingdom, while German speakers know the works primarily as *Die achtzehn Choräle*.

Because Klotz's edition contains all the chorale settings in the autograph, including the Canonic Variations, he gave his volume the generic title *Die Orgelchoräle aus der Leipziger Originalhandschrift* (The organ chorales from the Leipzig manuscript). The many organists who have since purchased the edition have naturally attached some importance to this appellation. Accordingly, it is not so unusual nowadays to en-counter concert programs and recordings that refer to the Great Eigh-teen as the "Leipzig Chorales."[24] The problem with this nickname, of course, is that none (or virtually none) of the settings were composed in Leipzig. Bach's "Leipzig Chorales" are Part III of the *Clavierübung*.

In the final analysis, "Great Eighteen" really says it all—and in rhyming fashion. For all eighteen of these works are truly "great" with respect to both their size and the quality of their music.

The best way to appreciate the structure of the collection is through a comparison. Of all of Bach's collections, printed or otherwise, it is Part III of the *Clavierübung* that shares the closest affinity with the Great Eighteen. Not only was it published around the same time that Bach began to compile the latter, but twenty-one of its twenty-seven pieces are organ chorales. Moreover, several of these pieces, like most of the Great Eighteen, represent large-scale, synthetic designs. Surely this print served as a major stimulus in the preparation of its counterpart.

According to recent research by Gregory Butler, the composition and engraving of Part III of the *Clavierübung* reach all the way back to 1735 or 1736, some three or four years before publication.[25] Hence, there can be no question about which of the two collections is earlier. By the time Bach began to notate the autograph of the Great Eighteen, around 1739 at the earliest, Part III of the *Clavierübung* was a fait ac-compli.

As Christoph Wolff has observed, Part III of the *Clavierübung* is Bach's first collection to display a cyclic order.[26] It opens with the great Prelude in E-flat Major and closes with the equally grand Fugue in E-flat Major (known as the "St. Anne"). Both movements are marked *pro Organo pleno*. Between these outer frames, the composer orders the twenty-one organ chorales in a variety of ways. (The remaining move-ments in the collection, the four Duetti, BWV 802–5, which appear between the final chorale and the E-flat fugue, need not concern us.)

For one thing, the chorales form a tightly knit liturgical design. The first nine set either the Kyrie or Gloria of the mass, while the last twelve are based on catechism texts. Within each of these two sections, Bach devotes two or three different organ settings to each of the ten chorale texts chosen. For example, within the mass section each of the three Kyrie texts ("Kyrie, Gott Vater in Ewigkeit," "Christe, aller Welt Trost," and "Kyrie, Gott Heiliger Geist") is arranged two different ways; the one Gloria text ("Allein Gott in der Höh sei Ehr") is the sub-ject of three settings. Whereas the three Gloria settings appear in di-rect succession, the Kyrie settings are split up into two groups of three works each. The first such group contains large *pedaliter* settings of each of the three Kyrie texts; the second group includes small *manualiter* settings of each.

Meanwhile, each of the catechism texts ("Dies sind die heilgen Zehn Gebot," "Wir glauben all an einen Gott," "Vater unser im Himmelreich," "Christ, unser Herr, zum Jordan kam," "Aus tiefer Not schrei ich zu dir," and "Jesus Christus, unser Heiland") is set twice, and the two settings always appear back-to-back. The first setting in each pair is a large *pedaliter* work; the second, a relatively small *manualiter* setting.

The three groups that contain three works are especially noteworthy, as each of them is unified by a different compositional technique. In the first (the *pedaliter* settings of the Kyrie), the position of the hymn tune descends from one work to the next in the order soprano–tenor–bass. In the second (the *manualiter* settings of the Kyrie), the three works form a metrical progression from simple triple to compound duple to compound triple. And in the third (the three Gloria settings), the tonality ascends from work to work in the order F major–G major–A major. All three devices make for a compelling musical sequence.

Clearly, Bach attempted to capture aspects of this structure in the Great Eighteen. The work that commences the collection—the "fantasy" on "Komm, Heiliger Geist"—is as majestic an organ chorale as has ever been conceived. Like the E-flat prelude, it is designated "for full organ" (*in Organo pleno*); it is also one of the longest works in the set. To quote Robert Marshall, "The first few measures of the opening composition . . . evoke at once the sense of monumentality and grandeur that Bach was striving for in this collection."[27]

Two correspondences between this work and the seventeenth chorale ("Komm, Gott Schöpfer") led Klotz to conclude that the Great Eighteen are every bit as cyclic as Part III of the *Clavierübung*.[28] For both works are marked *Organo pleno*, like the E-flat prelude and fugue from the *Clavierübung*, and both are Pentecost chorales whose incipits invoke the Holy Ghost. In addition, the texts of both hymns were authored by Martin Luther himself.[29] Of course, assuming that Bach did not authorize the inclusion of the seventeenth chorale, these two cases are hardly analogous. But it is tempting to believe nonetheless that Altnikol chose "Komm, Gott Schöpfer" as his final entry because of its hymnological correspondences to "Komm, Heiliger Geist." He may have added the *in Organo pleno* inscription himself to enhance the sense of cyclic structure that obtains between the first and seventeenth chorales.

A more fundamental analogy between these two collections is that the Great Eighteen also include, in four instances, multiple arrangements of the same chorale. As is usually the case in the *Clavierübung*, whenever a chorale is set more than once the two or three different arrangements appear in consecutive order. Parallels also exist within these groups. For example, between the three settings of "Nun komm" and "Allein Gott" the hymn melody migrates from soprano to bass, just as in the three *pedaliter* Kyrie chorales. (Moreover, the three "Allein Gott" settings, like those in the *Clavierübung*, are unified by means of a modulating key scheme, but here Bach uses the symmetrical disposition of A major–G major–A major.) This same progression also exists between the variations of the two chorale partitas from the Great Eighteen, "O Lamm Gottes" and "Komm, Gott Schöpfer."

With one exception, these are either groups of three works or works that consist of three variations. And in the case of the three *pedaliter* settings of the Kyrie, one can easily believe that Bach used this descending voice sequence to symbolize the Holy Trinity, just as he employs theological symbolism throughout his sacred music. As this sequence unfolds—in conjunction with three chorale texts devoted to, respectively, God the Father, God the Son, and God the Holy Ghost—it may well relate the story of the Triune God. In the first setting ("Kyrie, God and Father in Eternity"), the chorale tune appears in the highest voice to depict God the heavenly Father; in the second ("Christe, Consolation of All the World"), the melody moves down to an inner voice to portray God's earthly incarnation as Jesus; and in the third ("Kyrie, God, Holy Ghost"), the melody shifts down even further to the lowest, darkest voice to symbolize the Holy Spirit, the last (chronologically) and most mysterious member of the triumvirate.

The same argument may be made for two of the chorale trilogies from the Great Eighteen, especially that on "Allein Gott," whose four stanzas constitute a paean to the Holy Trinity. Stanza 1 serves as an encomium to God in general, while the second, third, and fourth stanzas address, respectively, the Father, Son, and Holy Ghost. It is not so far-fetched to think of the three settings from the Great Eighteen as representing Stanzas 2–4. As in the *Clavierübung*, "Allein Gott" receives three settings no doubt because of the hymn's Trinitarian text.[30]

In the case of the "Nun komm" trilogy, we are on shakier ground, since this Advent hymn naturally dwells on Jesus. Still, Stanza 2 focuses on the Holy Ghost, and Stanzas 5–6 center around God the Father. Most significant, the final stanza sets the famous text known as the Lesser Doxology, which begins with the exclamation "Glory be to the Father and to the Son and to the Holy Ghost."

Quite aside from any Trinitarianism, Bach must have found this downward progression engaging on purely musical grounds, too, and especially effective on the organ pedals. No listener can deny the climactic effect of saving a final statement of a melody for the bottom register. And because pedal stops typically include sixteen-foot registers or lower, they can carry the sound right down into the nether regions.

As regards the two groups of dual settings, "Komm, Heiliger Geist" and "Jesus Christus, unser Heiland," the latter recalls the chorale pairs from the *Clavierübung* in terms of both its *pedaliter-manualiter* ordering and the hint of a large–small succession. Was Altnikol also influenced by these factors? It may or may not be significant that this hymn appears toward the end of the Great Eighteen, just as it does in the *Clavierübung*.

And so, Part III of the *Clavierübung* served the Great Eighteen as a model with regard to its opening gesture, its preference for multiple settings of a single chorale, its use of certain musical devices to organize these multiple settings into groups, and its choice of particular hymns. Just as telling as these parallels, though, are some striking differences suggestive of a complementary relationship.

Consider, for instance, that the two collections are quite distinct in the chorale types they employ (although they do both favor synthetic forms derived from the cantus firmus chorale and chorale trio). While the *Clavierübung* contains no fewer than seven specimens of the chorale fughetta—a brief fugue on the opening phrase of the chorale—the Great Eighteen contain none. Also completely absent from the later collection but represented in the *Clavierübung* by two large-scale works is the chorale canon, a canonic rendering of the entire chorale tune. Conversely, the ornamental chorale, which is the most common chorale type in the Great Eighteen, is not to be found in the earlier collection. The same goes for the chorale motet. These statistics imply that in compiling the Great Eighteen Bach purposely chose certain chorale types (the ornamental chorale and the chorale motet) because he had not used them in the *Clavierübung* and that he purposely avoided others (the chorale fughetta and chorale canon) because he had used them there.

The most important of these statistics, as they relate to the Great Eighteen, are the complete absence of the chorale fughetta and the presence of seven ornamental chorales. Since Bach completely eschewed the chorale fughetta (and other small forms such as the melody chorale) in this collection, it has a very different rhythm. The seven fughettas in the *Clavierübung* result in a large–small alternation throughout the chorale section of the print; in the Great Eighteen, one large setting follows another.

Concerning the seven ornamental chorales in the collection, the five non-trio settings are among Bach's most lyrical creations. This songlike quality also stands in sharp contrast to the *Clavierübung*. For rather than the lavish decoration of dancelike tunes—just think of the trilogy of sarabandes from the Great Eighteen—it is the assimilation of Renaissance polyphony that so distinguishes the earlier collection.[31] Since Bach tends to employ this antiquated style in the *Clavierübung* for hymns that originated as plainchants, the sense of anachronism is all the greater. Closely tied to this phenomenon are the two canonic settings from the earlier collection, since they partake of a technique most typical of Renaissance or even Medieval music.

The presence of these obsolete styles, along with the high proportion of chorale tunes based on the old church modes, has earned for Part III of the *Clavierübung* such pejoratives as "austere" and "academic." Bach himself even called attention to the erudite quality of the collection by dedicating it to "Music Lovers and especially . . . Connoisseurs." Without question, the musical style of the Great Eighteen makes them a more accessible (and popular) group of pieces. Furthermore, most of their chorale tunes are unequivocally tonal and in the bright, major mode as well (only one major-mode melody is set in the *Clavierübung*). Could it be that Bach intended these settings for a wider, more dilettante audience?

Because they contain *de tempore* chorales, the Great Eighteen have always been of more utility as well. What self-respecting church organist here or abroad has not played the first setting of "Komm, Heiliger Geist" on Pentecost Sunday, or the first setting of "Nun komm" during Advent, or the partita on "O Lamm Gottes" during Passiontide?

Bach did not arrange these *de tempore* chorales according to the church year. Nor do the Great Eighteen display any recognizable liturgical design. Still, as we have seen vis-à-vis Part III of the *Clavierübung*, the works themselves follow an order that is hardly arbitrary. Let us continue by discussing further ways in which Bach organized the collection.

An obvious point of departure is the unit formed by the second setting of "Komm, Heiliger Geist" and the chorales on "An Wasserflüssen Babylon" and "Schmücke dich" (nos. 2–4). All three are ornamental chorales, and they all employ triple meter, in the manner of a sarabande, even though these chorale tunes were normally set in duple. Observe, too, that the positioning of the chorale tune creates a symmetrical soprano–tenor–soprano scheme. Moreover, the chorale tunes of the first two works are remarkably similar, which, given the other analogies, leads to remarkably similar figuration.[32] Just as the first two works in the manuscript form a hymnological pair—they are settings of the same hymn—the second, third, and fourth comprise a trio with respect to musical style.

The next twelve works are easy to summarize. After two seemingly unrelated settings (nos. 5–6) appear two consecutive works (nos. 7–8) that are both cantus firmus chorales. Each of the next eight settings (nos. 9–16) belongs to a group of works devoted to a single chorale.

It is important to remember that the second setting of "Allein Gott" (no. 13) concludes the first chronological phase of the autograph and that Bach waited at least four years before notating the third setting. Therefore, what one might think of as the original version of the collection included thirteen works that began and ended with a pair of settings of a single chorale.

Even at this preliminary stage, we can recognize a strong kinship between the "Nun komm" and "Allein Gott" groups. The first settings in each are ornamental chorales that, as discussed in chapter 1, borrow liberally from Italian violin figuration. Each of these works, in turn, is followed by an arrangement that conflates the chorale trio and ornamental chorale. With the addition of the third "Allein Gott" setting, the affinity between the two groups is made even stronger. For as the collection stands, each group begins with an ornamental chorale that places the hymn melody in the soprano; continues with a work that combines the chorale trio and ornamental chorale; and ends with a setting that shifts the hymn tune down to the bass voice, in the manner of a cantus firmus chorale. Because the two groups are side by side, they comprise a unit of six works altogether (nos. 9–14), by far the largest subgroup in the collection.

The last four settings (nos. 15–18) commence with Bach's final entry, the *pedaliter* "Jesus Christus, unser Heiland." If the inscription *in pleno Organo* in J. G. Walther's copy of the early version is authentic, Bach may have entered the work here to complement the full-organ setting that opens the collection, thus imparting to his fifteen entries some sense of cyclic structure. It should also be mentioned that the two "Jesus Christus" settings form a musical as well as hymnological unit, since they are both chorale motets. Whether this was a factor in Altnikol's choice of the second setting is of course open to speculation. That numbers 17 and 18 both originated within the *Orgelbüchlein* is probably just a coincidence.

Our findings on the structure of the Great Eighteen as a collection are summarized in Table 3-1. The data enclosed in rectangles demonstrate that most of the works are related to their neighbors either hymnologically or musically. These relationships, however, do not amount

TABLE 3-1 The Collective Structure of the Great Eighteen Chorales

BWV No.	Title	Chorale Type	Position of Chorale Tune	Other
651	"Komm, Heiliger Geist, Herre Gott"	cantus firmus chorale	bass (pedal)	
652	"Komm, Heiliger Geist, Herre Gott"	chorale motet / ornamental chorale	soprano	imitates sarabande
653	"An Wasserflüssen Babylon"	ornamental chorale	tenor	imitates sarabande
654	"Schmücke dich, o liebe Seele"	ornamental chorale	soprano	imitates sarabande
655	"Herr Jesu Christ, dich zu uns wend"	chorale trio / cantus firmus chorale	bass (pedal)	
656	"O Lamm Gottes, unschuldig"	chorale partita	Var. 1, soprano / Var. 2, alto / Var. 3, bass (pedal)	
657	"Nun danket alle Gott"	cantus firmus chorale	soprano	
658	"Von Gott will ich nicht lassen"	cantus firmus chorale	tenor (pedal)	
659	"Nun komm, der Heiden Heiland"	ornamental chorale	soprano	imitates Italian violin figuration
660	"Nun komm, der Heiden Heiland"	ornamental chorale / chorale trio	soprano	
661	"Nun komm, der Heiden Heiland"	cantus firmus chorale	bass (pedal)	
662	"Allein Gott in der Höh sei Ehr"	ornamental chorale	soprano	imitates Italian violin figuration
663	"Allein Gott in der Höh sei Ehr"	ornamental chorale / chorale trio	tenor	
664	"Allein Gott in der Höh sei Ehr"	chorale trio / cantus firmus chorale	bass (pedal)	

BWV No.	Title	Chorale Type	Position of Chorale Tune	Other
665	"Jesus Christus, unser Heiland"	chorale motet		
666	"Jesus Christus, unser Heiland"	chorale motet		
667	"Komm, Gott Schöpfer, Heiliger Geist"	chorale partita	Var. 1, soprano Var. 2, bass (pedal)	
668	"Vor deinen Thron tret ich hiermit"	cantus firmus chorale	soprano	

to a structure that unifies the set as a whole. Such a structure simply does not present itself, no matter what one might read to the contrary. Considering the composer's well-known penchant for architectonic form, the Great Eighteen chorales suggest a work in progress—a work that, for whatever reasons, was never properly completed. But the fact that Bach assembled these gems into any kind of a collection imbues them with a manifold significance that otherwise would not exist.

Chapter 4

THE MUSIC AND ITS PERFORMANCE

———————————— ✿ ————————————

*N*ow that we have studied the Great Eighteen as a collection, let us reconsider them as individual works. Our purpose here will be to examine aspects of the music not touched on in previous chapters, particularly issues of performance practice. We will cover the pieces in their order of appearance in the autograph manuscript. Not surprisingly, this is the same sequence found in the *Bach-Werke-Verzeichnis*.

Each commentary is preceded by the work's heading more or less exactly as it appears in the autograph, with the individual lines separated by a solidus (/). Incredibly, these headings have yet to be accurately reproduced in any publication.

"KOMM, HEILIGER GEIST, HERRE GOTT" (COME, HOLY GHOST, LORD GOD), BWV 651

Autograph Heading: *J. J. Fantasia sup[er] Kom heiliger Geist. canto fermo in Pedal. di J S Bach. / In Organo pleno*

Nowhere does the text of this Pentecost hymn refer to that event as recorded in Acts 2.[1] But the exuberance of Bach's "fantasy," with its whirling manual figuration and full-organ registration, is entirely compatible with such imagery as rushing winds and tongues of fire. The late Glenn Gould even chose the piece, as recorded by Marie-Claire Alain, for the concluding fireworks scene of the film *Slaughterhouse Five*. This is one of Bach's longest organ chorales, and performances typically run about six minutes. A relatively slow tempo can easily add two minutes to the count.[2]

The beginning and end of the work are highly unusual for a cantus firmus chorale in which the pedals state the hymn melody, for here the pedals start and finish with free material instead. In no other Bach composition of this type do the pedals begin with anything but the first note of the chorale tune, and in only two others (the trio on "Herr Jesu Christ" from the Great Eighteen and the *Fuga sopra il Magnificat*, BWV 733) do they conclude with anything but the last note of the tune.

The pedals could easily have been delayed until measure 8, where the hymn melody commences. An opening tonic pedal point, though, creates an infinitely more powerful effect, and one familiar from many of the composer's free organ preludes (see BWV 537, 540, 546, 562, 568, and 569). Similarly, Bach could have concluded with a tonic triad on the downbeat of measure 104. But the ending he ultimately settled on is much stronger, because both the V and I chords are set as whole notes in root position, and far more dramatic as well. Particularly striking is the transition between the second and third beats of measure 104, where contrary motion between the soprano and bass in their outermost registers leads to a secondary diminished-seventh chord.

As various older editions show, it was once customary to herald the chorale tune by adding pedal stops in measure 8.[3] Such an alteration, however, serves only to disrupt the musical flow. The performer should feel no need to change registration—or manuals—anywhere in this piece, not even in the concluding "Hallelujah" section. Adding stops in measure 89 would be messy business indeed.

Bach's registration instruction, of course, should not be taken literally. From what is known about Baroque practice, *Organo pleno* merely implied all principal and mixture stops, plus optional pedal reeds.[4] The modern player might consider adding a Sesquialtera, since mixture stops on Thuringian organs of this period typically contained third-sounding pipes throughout their compass.[5] Ideally, this addition will help clarify the dense fugal texture.

"KOMM, HEILIGER GEIST, HERRE GOTT" (COME, HOLY GHOST, LORD GOD), BWV 652

Autograph Heading: *Komm heiliger Geist. alio modo. à 2 Clav. et Ped. di J. S. Bach.*

This second setting of "Komm, Heiliger Geist" is Bach's only organ chorale to combine the chorale motet and ornamental chorale. Again, the unusually long hymn melody appears complete, with each of the nine phrases serving as a point of imitation. The result is no fewer than 199 bars of music, which makes this the second longest organ chorale Bach ever wrote (the longest is "Herr Gott, dich loben wir," BWV 725). Not only are all the phrases set imitatively; they also follow the same voice order (tenor–alto–bass–soprano) and key sequence (tonic–dominant–tonic–tonic), and they all end with the same rhythm, a trilled dotted quarter note followed by two sixteenths. This monotony may be just as responsible for the work's neglect as its great length. Still, the music is beautiful beyond words.

Those stalwarts who last the full nine minutes are rewarded, beginning in measure 187, with a lively free coda that suddenly transforms the mood from supplication to ecstasy (see Example 4-1). While the coda doubtless depicts the word "Hallelujah," which concludes all three stanzas of the text, the final phrase of the chorale tune actually ends (on the downbeat of m. 187) just before the coda begins. One is reminded of Bach's Weimar organ pupil Johann Gotthilf Ziegler and his report that "as concerns the playing of chorales, I was instructed by my teacher, Capellmeister Bach . . . not to play the songs merely offhand but according to the sense [*Affect*] of the words."[6]

EXAMPLE 4-1. "Komm, Heiliger Geist, Herre Gott," BWV 652

"AN WASSERFLÜSSEN BABYLON"
(BY THE WATERS OF BABYLON), BWV 653

Autograph Heading: *Am Waßer / Flüßen / Babylon / a 2 Clav. / et /*
Pedal di / J. S. Bach.

The text of this hymn is a translation of Psalm 137, a moving lament on the Babylonian Exile of the Jews. Bach's choice of the sarabande as a compositional model recalls his appropriation of that dance type for the final elegiac choruses of the St. John and St. Matthew Passions. The sorrowful *Affekt* of the organ chorale is especially palpable from measure 48 on, owing to an increased use of chromaticism and the minor mode (see, for instance, the cross-relations in mm. 67 and 76).

As a bar-form chorale, "An Wasserflüssen" poses quite an anomaly to Bach's normal practice, for in those relatively few instances where he actually notated the restatement of the *Stollen*, he tended to vary the material from its original presentation. Here, though, the restatement is fully notated, in both the early and late versions (BWV 653a and 653, respectively), with virtually the same material as the initial statement. Besides the missing soprano trill in measure 23 of the late version, the only discrepancies occur between measures 12–14 and 24–26, that is, at the very end of the *Stollen*. Perhaps when Bach composed the piece he intended to vary the restatement but did not realize until measure 24 that he had copied the *Stollen* note for note. Although he chose not to go back and alter measures 19–23, he might well have performed this passage with improvised variations, in accordance with the Baroque practice of the varied reprise. Performers today might do likewise.

This work may also be connected to one of Bach's most famous organ performances, that given in Hamburg in 1720 on the fifty-eight-stop organ of St. Catherine's Church. According to his obituary, he played in front of a select audience for more than two hours, improvising for nearly half an hour on the chorale "An Wasserflüssen Babylon."[7] Among those in attendance was the church's elderly organist, Johann Adam Reinken. One of Reinken's best-known works is a massive organ fantasy on this same chorale, a fact, according to the obituary, not unknown to Bach.[8] Since the obituary states that the chorale was chosen by "those present" and not by Bach himself, Reinken may have requested this particular melody to test the improvisational skills of his junior colleague. Of course, Bach passed the exam with flying colors, and afterward Reinken said to him, "I thought that this art was dead, but I see that in you it still lives."[9]

Considering the strong influence of Reinken on the young Bach,[10] he very likely knew Reinken's fantasy (and not merely the fact that Reincken had written such a piece). Thus, while extemporizing on the tune Bach could have purposely aimed for a rendition just as variegated and grandiose. He may also somehow have incorporated into this "improvisation" his only extant organ setting of this hymn, which in 1720 would have meant the early version, BWV 653a. About twenty years later, when Bach revised this work for inclusion in the Great Eighteen, he tacked on a seven-bar coda that closes with the same highly unusual gesture as Reinken's fantasy: a descending scale in the ornamental solo voice (see Examples 4-2 and 4-3). It is hard not to believe that this correspondence represents an act of homage.

When, in his twilight years, Bach set about revising this organ chorale, he must have thought fondly about this epsiode in his life. Thinking of the organ at St. Catherine's alone would have brought back pleasant memories, as he was particularly enamored of its reed stops.[11] Would he have played the solo line on a soft reed stop, as is the custom nowadays? Whatever the answer, performing the work in this manner—despite its use of the *Tierce en Taille* as a model—provides a meaningful link to the Hamburg performance.

To return to the coda, its last four bars are surely the richest passage in the entire work. Here Bach combines a final statement of the ritor-

EXAMPLE 4-2. Johann Adam Reinken, "An Wasserflüssen Babylon"

EXAMPLE 4-3. "An Wasserflüssen Babylon," BWV 653

nello in the soprano, a second pedal line in ascending motion, and a descending scale in the left hand. The major seventh between the two pedal lines in the penultimate measure creates great tension, and its resolution in contrary motion with the descending scale could not be more satisfying. Precisely at the point of resolution, the ritornello also ends.

"SCHMÜCKE DICH, O LIEBE SEELE" (ADORN YOURSELF, O DEAR SOUL), BWV 654

Autograph Heading: *Schmücke / dich, o liebe / Seele. / a 2 Clav. et / Pedal / di J. S. Bach*

The text of this chorale has been described as a "rapturous meditation" on the rite of communion.[12] Bach sets the hymn as an ornamental chorale and uses ornamentation within the ritornello as a pun on the word *schmücke* ("adorn").

No one would dispute that "Schmücke dich" is one of the most beloved chorale settings ever written by any composer—or that it possesses a mystical charm that can move even the most obstinate listener.

The tune itself is very lyrical, especially the two ascents to the upper-octave tonic pitch, and Bach's tendency in the middle voices toward stepwise eighth notes in parallel thirds and sixths leads to a euphony few would associate with him. (The accompanimental figuration comes remarkably close to that of Variation 10 of Bach's organ partita on "Sei gegrüsset, Jesu gütig," a movement also based on the sarabande.) Let us not forget, either, the gorgeous coloratura writing for the soprano voice, particularly the climax tones in measures 15, 29, 88, and 103.

"Schmücke dich" is also a bar-form chorale. But here, in contrast to the previous piece, Bach indicates the restatement of the *Stollen* by repeat marks only. The player can vary the restatement merely by changing registration, but this still means a note-for-note repeat.[13] An infinitely more interesting approach is to add ornamentation on the repeat, much as singers do on the repeat of the "A" section in da capo arias and as harpsichordists do in binary dance movements.

This setting is a prime candidate for such treatment primarily because the soprano occupies its own manual. Since the right hand plays this part only, without ever taking the alto, it is free to embellish at will. Regardless of how far the soprano might descend in the midst of any added embellishment, the alto voice will never obstruct it; the hands will never cross on the same manual. The slow rhythms in the soprano also greatly facilitate the addition of ornaments, as does the slow tempo dictated by the use of the sarabande as a compositional model. Besides, a note-for-note repeat of such a lengthy passage—about two minutes' worth—would tempt even the most conscientious player to omit the repeat altogether.[14]

As an example to be followed, consider George Ritchie's recent recording (see Example 4-4).[15] He tends to decorate only where a half note or dotted half note sits alone, and twice by means of the same motive (♩♪♪♪) Bach himself employs throughout the soprano voice. Thus, Ritchie's added ornamentation not only relieves points of stasis in the melody; it also heightens the sense of motivic unity within the line.

Those players who are reticent about adding their own ornamentation have two other options. The first is to simplify Bach's notated ornamentation for the first statement of the *Stollen* and restore it all on the repeat.[16] This, in fact, is precisely what Ritchie does with the compound trill in measure 15 by omitting the appoggiatura the first time through. The second is to employ in succession the two different forms of ornamentation found between the early and late versions of the work. Marie-Claire Alain has recorded "Schmücke dich" in just this way.[17]

EXAMPLE 4-4. "Schmücke dich, o liebe Seele," BWV 654. George Ritchie's ornamentation of Bach's soprano line (as transcribed by the author).

"HERR JESU CHRIST, DICH ZU UNS WEND" (LORD JESUS CHRIST, TURN TO US), BWV 655

Autograph Heading: *Trio sup[er] / Herr Jesu Xst, / dich zu uns wend. / a 2 Clav. et / Pedal di / J. S. Bach*

In this heading, the Greek letter "Χ" (= Chi) stands for "Chri[st]."[18] Because of its shape, the letter also signifies the cross on which Jesus was crucified. This abbreviation appears frequently in Bach's autograph manuscripts, and it is of course characteristic of Christian tradition in general.

Here we have a decidedly effervescent work, one whose overall sonority has been likened to a carillon or glockenspiel.[19] As discussed in chapter 1, it begins as a free trio in ritornello form but later (in m. 52) becomes a cantus firmus chorale. Starting in measure 71, after presenting the entire chorale tune in the pedals, Bach adds two final ritornello statements.

The addition of a pedal stop for the hymn melody makes good musical sense and, due to the pedal rests in measures 51–52, is easy to accomplish. As for when the original registration should return, measure 71 offers two possibilities: between the first and second eighth notes (immediately after the last note of the chorale melody) or between the fifth and sixth eighth notes (immediately before the final two ritornello statements).

"O LAMM GOTTES, UNSCHULDIG"
(O LAMB OF GOD, INNOCENTLY SLAUGHTERED),
BWV 656

Autograph Heading: *O Lam Gottes / unschuldig. / 3 Versus. / di / J. S. Bach / 1 Versus. manualiter*

In what may be a unique hymnological case, the three stanzas of this Passiontide chorale contain essentially the same words. But whereas the first two stanzas conclude with: "Have mercy on us, Jesus," the third ends with: "Give us your peace, Jesus." Bach mirrors this tripartite structure by writing exactly three variations and by depicting the last two lines of text, in Variation 3, in dramatic fashion. For the penultimate line, "Otherwise, we would have had to despair," intensely chromatic harmonies appear out of nowhere, whereas for the final line ("Give us your peace, Jesus") the figuration switches abruptly to rapid scales. Spitta hailed the piece as a "marvel of profoundly religious art!"[20]

"O Lamm Gottes" is unquestionably one of Bach's most popular organ chorales. Taken as a whole, however, the three variations of this "continuous" partita make a distinctly uneven impression. Variation 3 seems consistently inspired—and, as we will see, not just with regard to text painting. But the first two variations are quite conventional and monochromatic, at least in terms of their figuration.

Both are based on the same accompanimental motive, three off-the-beat eighth notes followed by a fourth note of equal or greater value. Known as the *suspirans* (because it begins with a "suspiration"), this is the most common of all Baroque keyboard figures. Since it sounds constantly, the motive produces continuous eighth-note motion throughout the first two variations. The *suspirans* is also Bach's favorite accompanimental idea in the *Orgelbüchlein*. But there he is working with an extremely compact design, one without an introduction or interludes between the phrases of the chorale. In the present work, the chorale tune proper does not enter until measure 10, and Variation 2 contains a lengthy interlude at its midpoint (mm. 64–68). This interlude, more-over, is little more than one gigantic sequence, and one of the most repetitive the composer ever wrote.[21] There is also the fact that in nei-ther of these variations did Bach bother to write a varied reprise of the *Stollen*. On several different levels, then, the amount of repetition is considerable.

Variation 3 begins according to a very different plan. A pedal line is added to carry the chorale melody, the meter changes from $\frac{3}{2}$ to $\frac{9}{4}$, the *suspirans* is replaced with quarter notes, and the second note of the hymn tune is raised to d-sharp.[22] What is more, the *Stollen* receives a varied restatement in which the accompaniment begins an octave higher. From this point on, basically each of the remaining phrases is paired with a different accompanimental motive. (Note in particular how the descending chromatic motive used for the penultimate phrase is ingeniously woven into the *pedaliter* chorale line.) Bach also adds a fourth voice in the middle of the chromatic passage (mm. 136–39) and a fifth in the last three bars. By means of these added parts, the work culminates in a mighty crescendo that seems to grow all the way to the end of the last rising scale.

Despite these discrepancies, "O Lamm Gottes" is still a work whose three variations comprise a loosely unified whole. Just consider the de-scending voice order (soprano–alto–bass) used systematically from one variation to the next for the presentation of the chorale melody. Bach also employs the same sort of *style brisé* figuration between Vari-ations 1 and 2 as between Variations 2 and 3 (in the latter instance, ending with a pungent tonic–dominant clash). A further cohering fac-tor is the return of the *suspirans*, in the context of $\frac{3}{2}$ time, for the final phrase of Variation 3 (the scale figures here constitute two successive statements of this motive). As Werner Breig has observed, this material functions both as a coda for Variation 3 and as a reprise for the entire composition.[23]

Most players sensibly change registration between variations, along the lines of a gradual crescendo, and such a buildup greatly enhances the climactic nature of Variation 3. The addition of stops within this variation, particularly for the last phrase, is also effective. As we will see in the next chapter, an early advocate of both of these techniques was Felix Mendelssohn.

As for tempo, the same half-note pulse should be maintained through-out all three variations. The chromatic passage in Variation 3 is often taken twice as slow as the material on either side of it, presumably to underscore the dissonant harmony. But a ritenuto here does little more than fragment the penultimate phrase of the hymn tune.

"NUN DANKET ALLE GOTT"
(LET EVERYONE NOW THANK GOD), BWV 657

Autograph Heading: *Nun dancket alle Gott. a 2 Clav. et Ped.*
canto fermo in Soprano. di J. S. Bach.

In this instance, we find Bach's only organ setting of the famous hymn better known to English speakers as "Now Thank We All Our God." As discussed in chapter 1, the compositional model is a type of cantus firmus chorale created by Pachelbel. According to Spitta, Bach surpasses this model through "tuneful counterpoint."[24] One might add that the counterpoint is also extraordinarily busy and quite difficult to perform, especially in the many passages where the left hand has to take both inner voices.

It has long been the custom to play the soprano chorale melody on a strong eight-foot reed, either alone or in combination with a unison or octave principal. As Thomas Harmon has argued, players would do well to consider the latter option in light of how Bach treats this same hymn in the opening chorus of Cantata 192, *Nun danket alle Gott.*[25] There, too, the hymn is the subject of a cantus firmus chorale, with the chorale tune sung by the sopranos, doubled by oboes. As Harmon points out, this is a type of registration recommended by Bach's pupil Johann Friedrich Agricola.

"VON GOTT WILL ICH NICHT LASSEN"
(FROM GOD I DO NOT WANT TO LEAVE), BWV 658

Autograph Heading: *Von Gott will ich [nicht] laßen. canto fermo in*
pedal. di J. S. Bach.[26]

With language suspiciously similar to Robert Schumann's characterization of "Schmücke dich" (see next chapter), Spitta maintained that the accompanimental voices of this work "wind around and above [the chorale tune] like a luxurious garland of amaranth."[27] This is, to be sure, an exquisite composition, and one that feels under the fingers rather like one of Bach's harpsichord sinfonias (BWV 787–801).

Especially memorable are the two penultimate measures, where both the alto and the left-hand bass part are assigned new material (see Example 4-5). Although notated in faster rhythms, the alto gives the effect of syncopated eighth notes on b'-flat (𝄽♪♪𝄽♪♪), whereas the bass moves according to a falling-octave motive, which, if memory serves, the late Anton Heiller likened to the beating of the human heart. The tension in the penultimate bar itself between the leading-tone diminished-seventh

EXAMPLE 4-5. "Von Gott will ich nicht lassen," BWV 658

chord and double tonic pedal point is almost unbearable. As Peter Williams observes, the passage is unnecessary from the perspective of phrase structure.[28] But the piece would be greatly diminished without it.

Bach notates the pedal line that carries the hymn tune in the tenor rather than bass range, a unique occurrence among the Great Eighteen chorales. But at what pitch should the part be played? The practice of using a four-foot stop goes all the way back to the alleged Bach pupil Johann Christoph Oley, whose inscription *Pedal 4 fuss* appears in his manuscript copy of this work.[29] This registration might well project the melody in a way that an eight-foot stop cannot, yet it also annihilates the tenor voice, creating instead two alto parts. Still, as Clark Kelly has pointed out, an eight-foot pedal stop, if combined with an eight-foot manual registration, can lead to such dubious results as parallel fifths between the pedal and alto parts in measure 30, between the second and third beats (see Example 4-6).[30] Whichever pitch one chooses, the overall tone and balance of the registration should obviously be taken into account as well.

As for other performance matters, users of the Peters and Breitkopf editions should add an a-flat sixteenth note on the repeat of measure 1. Although written in tiny script (as a direct) and crowded onto the end of the left-hand staff after the first ending, this note is visible in the autograph manuscript.

The autograph does not indicate any kind of break in the pedal part before the last phrase, which begins at the pickup to measure 34, and therefore no edition gives this instruction. In order to preserve the phrase structure of the original chorale, however, the e-flat in measure 34 should be shortened. This is not a problem elsewhere in the piece because all other adjacent phrases either are separated by rests or end and begin on the same pitch. In the latter instances, these repeated notes automatically separate the two phrases.

EXAMPLE 4-6. "Von Gott will ich nicht lassen," BWV 658

"NUN KOMM, DER HEIDEN HEILAND"
(COME NOW, SAVIOR OF THE HEATHEN),
BWV 659

Autograph Heading: *Nun kom / der Heÿ / den Heÿ= / land. /*
a 2 Clav. / et Ped. / di / J. S. Bach

Here Bach gives us the first of three arrangements of this famous Advent chorale. It remains one of his most popular organ works, period, due both to the arabesquelike figuration in the soprano that embellishes the hymn melody and to the rich accompanimental material that sounds beneath. Harvey Grace singled out the piece unequivocally as the composer's "most beautiful" organ chorale of all.[31]

As we will discuss, the work also projects a deep sense of mysticism quite in keeping with the theme of Christ's Incarnation. This may be why it is played (by the late Fernando Germani) during the "adoption" scene toward the end of Ermanno Olmi's film *L'albero degli zoccoli* (The tree of wooden clogs). In this scene, the day after a young couple have just spent their first night together as husband and wife they decide to take in an abandoned boy offered to them by a nun. Considering the film's emphasis on "simple Christian steadfastness,"[32] the parallels to Joseph, Mary, the baby Jesus, and God's gift of the Messiah are undeniable.

As mentioned in chapter 1, each of the four soprano phrases begins as if it would run about two bars but winds up lasting two or three times this long. In each case, the first three or four notes of the phrase appear more or less as quarter notes, only to be followed by rising sequences completely unrelated to the tune. Not until the last note of each phrase, evidently, does the original chorale serve again as a point of reference. Thus, the intervening three or four notes, although they are all touched upon at some juncture, are effectively lost. This must be what Hermann Keller had in mind when he wrote that this piece "has a fantastic beauty that we never perceive fully."[33]

One must look hard indeed to find another ornamental chorale by Bach in which the hymn tune is treated so freely. (The only candidate is the second setting of "Allein Gott" from the Great Eighteen.) Rather astonishingly, it is absent from the soprano voice more often than not, as if to depict the great mystery of the Incarnation. Bach may also have had in mind the text that concludes the first stanza: "All the world is *amazed* that God gave him such a birth."

Example 4-7 illustrates the second phrase. Here Bach begins with a straightforward quarter-note rendition of the first three notes (g′–b′-flat–c″), then introduces a motive independent of the chorale melody (♪♪♪ ♪♪♪ ♩) and subjects it to exactly two rising sequences—for him, standard melodic construction. Additional free figuration follows and finally gives way to a half-note on b′-flat, the last note of the phrase. Precisely where the listener is supposed to hear the phrase's middle three notes (b′-flat–c″–d″) is far from clear.

EXAMPLE 4-7. "Nun komm, der Heiden Heiland," BWV 659

The material allotted to the inner voices throughout the work also adopts different guises, ranging from imitative (as in the opening pre-imitation of the first phrase) to homophonic. An example of the latter texture occurs in the penultimate measure of Example 4-7, where the left hand is reduced to eighth-note chords and rests. What strange music! Only the first chord is in root position, and all the tonic b-flat triads are merely implied by the d's in the pedal. To add to the uneasi-ness, the bass oscillates between e-flat and d, rather than moving for any length of time in one direction. Here, then, both the accompani-ment and the solo line lend an element of mysticism.

"NUN KOMM, DER HEIDEN HEILAND"
(COME NOW, SAVIOR OF THE HEATHEN),
BWV 660

Autograph Heading: *Trio. sup[er] / Nun kom der / Heyden Heÿland / a due Bassi / è canto fermo / di / J. S. Bach*

This second setting of "Nun komm" is something else entirely. Although the hymn tune once again appears in the soprano, surrounded by em-bellishment, it is now accompanied by two bass voices, one played by the left hand on a separate manual, the other played by the feet. In no other trio composition for any medium does Bach invert the standard scoring of two treble parts and bass.

In the context of this unique disposition, certain passages stand out as most peculiar. Take, for example, the first and last soprano phrases, which set the same melody. Since the half note functions as the stan-dard rhythm for the notes of the chorale tune, the listener expects each phrase to cadence two beats earlier. Also disorienting is how the music continues. In each instance, an abbreviated ritornello statement (using the same segment of the theme) leads to a four-voice eighth-note chord in the left hand. These chords themselves are a big surprise, since oth-erwise trio texture is strictly maintained. But they are doubly surpris-ing in the early version, because Bach indicates there by means of a wavy vertical line that each is to be arpeggiated, a highly unusual tech-nique in organ music (see Figure 4-1 for a complete facsimile of the au-tograph of the early version). These arpeggiated chords have also been marshaled as evidence that the left-hand part was originally for viola da gamba and, consequently, that the original version of this work complex is a lost cantata movement for solo soprano, gamba, and continuo.[34]

Each of these chords, in turn, is followed by more unusual material. After the first chord, which cadences in D minor, the music immediately shifts back to G minor, resulting in a most abrupt "modulation." Stranger still, after the second chord breaks off, in the last bar, a G pedal sounds by itself for an extra beat and a half until the very end of the piece.[35] One is not likely to find another work by Bach or anyone else that ends this way.

Little wonder, then, that Spitta denounced this setting as "startingly reckless" and "almost unapproachable in the abruptness of its character."[36] In a similar vein, Harvey Grace found the work "so dark in mood as to be repellent on first acquaintance."[37] He objected specifically to the dissonant intervals in the ritornello theme, the consistently low range, and what he perceived as a liberal use of harmonic dissonance. The lugubrious nature of the piece even suggested to Hermann Keller a depiction of Christ's descent into hell, as cited in the fifth stanza of the chorale text.[38]

For all these reasons, this work remains the least popular of the three "Nun komm" arrangements in the Great Eighteen. In addition, organists have shied away from the piece because it is by far the hardest of the three to perform. The fast, disjunct ritornello theme poses problems for the left hand as well as the feet, and playing just these two parts makes for an exacting technical exercise. Considering that a florid right-hand voice is superimposed, the work approaches outright virtuosity.[39]

Here we also have the only Great Eighteen chorale whose early version survives in an autograph manuscript (reproduced in Figure 4-1). As explained in chapter 2, although this source is subsumed under the same shelf number as Bach's autograph of the revised versions of the Great Eighteen chorales (SBB Mus. ms. Bach P 271), it originated decades earlier as a separate manuscript. The title page reads: "Nun komm der Heyden Heÿl: / á 2 Clav: et Ped: / di / Joh: Seb: Bach," the heading above the first page of music, "Nun komm der Heyden Heyland. á 2 Clav. & Pedal."[40]

To judge from several corrections and erasures, this manuscript is not a composing score or fair copy but a revision copy, just like most of the autograph entries of the revised versions of the Great Eighteen chorales.[41] Bach's script here seems much too neat for a first draft, and no revisions of a formative nature are to be found (the first statement of the complex canonic ritornello is entirely free of corrections). Elsewhere in the source, though, one encounters several revisions that can only be construed as compositional.

Two obvious instances occur in the top line at measures 17 (last system of the first page, first bar) and 35 (penultimate system of the second page, penultimate bar). As the large note heads show, the original reading in each case was merely a half note on b'-flat, representing a

FIGURE 4-1A. Autograph score of "Nun komm, der Heiden Heiland," BWV 660a, title page (Staatsbibliothek zu Berlin—Preussischer Kulturbesitz, Musikabteilung mit Mendelssohn-Archiv, Mus. ms. Bach P 271, p. 107)

FIGURE 4-1B. Autograph score of "Nun komm, der Heiden Heiland," BWV 660a, mm. 1–20 (Staatsbibliothek zu Berlin—Preussischer Kulturbesitz, Musik-abteilung mit Mendelssohn-Archiv, Mus. ms. Bach P 271, p. 108)

FIGURE 4-1C. Autograph score of "Nun komm, der Heiden Heiland," BWV 660a, mm. 21–40 (Staatsbibliothek zu Berlin—Preussischer Kulturbesitz, Musik-abteilung mit Mendelssohn-Archiv, Mus. ms. Bach P 271, p. 109)

FIGURE 4-1D. Autograph score of "Nun komm, der Heiden Heiland," BWV 660a, mm. 41–42 (Staatsbibliothek zu Berlin—Preussischer Kulturbesitz, Musikabteilung mit Mendelssohn-Archiv, Mus. ms. Bach P 271, p. 110)

single note of the hymn tune. The revised readings are also virtually the same, with a quarter note on b′-flat tied to a sixteenth, followed by three more sixteenths. Bach's original conception, then, involved a somewhat less ornate rendition of the chorale melody. We can also assume that his lost composing score contained only half notes here.

Interestingly, when the composer set out to revise this piece for inclusion in the Great Eighteen, he reworked the passage at measure 35, changing the pitches of the sixteenths—and reversing their direction—from d″–c″–b′-flat to a′–b′-flat–c″. He must have done this due to how poorly the last two sixteenths of the former reading jibe with the left-hand part (minor seventh moving to a perfect fifth). In the final version, parallel sixths prevail.

A different type of revision takes place in the series of pedal eighth notes at measures 23–24 (top system of the second page, third and fourth bars). There the pitches of at least four of the notes were changed. The large note head and thick stem of the second note indicate that it was originally at a lower pitch; the fourth note was originally d, judging from its extra note head; the note head of the sixth note extends through the staff line immediately above, suggesting that the original pitch was f; and the erased and rewritten staff lines above the seventh note show that it was originally higher. Bach apparently altered the fourth and sixth notes, once again, because of dissonances with the left-hand voice.

Noteworthy, too, is how the last four pedal eighth notes in measure 24 were revised in the final version of the work. The second and fourth notes were both transposed down a third, while the first was replaced with an eighth rest. The former changes create stronger, root-position chord progressions; the latter avoids repeated notes on c.

"NUN KOMM, DER HEIDEN HEILAND"
(COME NOW, SAVIOR OF THE HEATHEN),
BWV 661

Autograph Heading: *Nun kom der / Heyden Heÿland. / in Organo /*
pleno. canto / fermo in / Pedal / di / J. S. Bach.

After all the idiosyncrasies posed by its predecessor, the third "Nun komm" arrangement seems positively normal. The hymn tune now appears in the pedals without any embellishment other than neighboring and passing tones. Still, Bach handles the melody differently than one might expect.

The fact is that all four lines of the chorale text have seven syllables, implying a uniform, metric rhythm such as ♩♩♩♩|♩♩♩. This is the basic rhythm to which "Nun komm" was set in early eighteenth-century hymnals and in cantatas by Bach, Buxtehude, and others. But here only the interior phrases adopt this pattern. The exterior ones, which are melodically identical, follow the very unmetrical rhythm of ♩♩♩|♩♩♩|♩. Interestingly, Bach's *Orgelbüchlein* setting of this chorale displays the same inconsistency.

As discussed in chapter 1, the present work closely resembles that which opens the Great Eighteen, the Fantasia on "Komm, Heiliger Geist." Although Spitta found the latter piece "even more powerful," the former may actually be the superior composition.[42] To quote Harvey Grace, "It is shorter and more compact, and the chorale melody makes a better bass."[43]

"ALLEIN GOTT IN DER HÖH SEI EHR"
(ALONE TO GOD ON HIGH BE HONOR), BWV 662

Autograph Heading: *Allein Gott in der Höh seÿ Ehr. a 2 Clav. et Ped.*
canto fermo in Sopr. di J S. Bach / Adagio.

Bach follows the "Nun komm" trilogy with three renditions of the German Gloria. This tune must have been a favorite, since it appears in more of his extant organ chorales than any other hymn melody. Six settings are found in the Great Eighteen and Part III of the *Clavierübung*, and four miscellaneous arrangements survive as well (BWV 711, 715, 716, and 717).

Of these ten arrangements, the present work is especially beloved. For one thing, its melodies and harmonies are particularly pleasing: the subject of the fugal ritornello emphasizes the sweet sixth degree of the major scale; and as in "Schmücke dich," the middle voices often proceed in parallel thirds and sixths. Bach enhances this euphony with some of the most exquisite—and profuse—ornamentation he ever wrote. Indeed, this ranks as his most ornate chorale setting altogether. Not only is the solo line more florid than in any other Bach organ chorale, but so is the accompaniment. Twelve separate ornamental symbols appear in the first three measures alone, including appoggiatura "hooks," a turn, trills, and a slide (Example 1-3 gives this passage according to the somewhat less ornate early version). As André Pirro declared over a century ago, "No piece could be more elaborated than this one."[44] Nonetheless, owing to the relative paucity of free material, the chorale tune is still easier to recognize than in the first setting of "Nun komm."[45]

In the realm of performance practice, the autograph heading indicates a tempo of adagio, which is the first tempo marking encountered in our survey (this indication appears only in the revised version). As Robert Marshall has demonstrated, adagio was for Bach the slowest of the main tempo designations, slower even than largo.[46] A reasonable metronome setting—and one consistent with Marshall's findings—would be ♪ = 60.

On the subject of ornamentation, the custom in former times was to play the "hooked" appoggiaturas in the ritornello as thirty-seconds immediately before the next beat or half-beat (♪ ♪♪ ♪♪♪ ♪).[47] But based on what we now know about Baroque practice, these notes should no doubt be played in "Lombard" style, that is, ♪♪♪♪ ♪♪ ♪♪.

Finally, for most of the reasons cited previously in connection with "Schmücke dich," any performance of this sublime piece should feature a varied reprise of its *Stollen*, with alterations to the soprano line. Both George Ritchie and Joan Lippincott have recorded the work in this manner, on the Raven (OAR-300) and Gothic (G 49099) labels, respectively.

"ALLEIN GOTT IN DER HÖH SEI EHR" (ALONE TO GOD ON HIGH BE HONOR), BWV 663

Autograph Heading: *Allein Gott in / der Höh seÿ / Ehr. /*
a 2 Clav. et Ped. / canto fermo in Tenore /
di J. S. Bach. / Cantabile

Bach now sets the chorale as a trio, but one whose free voice leading often encompasses four and five voices. The combination of these thick textures with nonstop eighth notes in the ritornello and in the embellished chorale tune makes for an extraordinarily busy composition. In no other ornamental chorale by Bach is the ornamentation accomplished by means of such motoric figuration. More important, this figuration renders the hymn melody virtually unrecognizable to the ear. All this activity suggested to Spitta "a tropical luxuriance of foliage with many-colored blossoms," while Hermann Keller dismissed the work as "a jungle in which a listener can hardly find his way."[48] Thicket or not, the piece does not enjoy great popularity.

Despite this neglect—which is totally undeserved—this work offers some highly interesting issues for the performer. For example, in measure 15 of the revised version, beat 2, Bach draws in the autograph what looks like a wavy arpeggiation line between g′ and e″.[49] Because of the rarity of such symbols in organ music, editors have either ignored

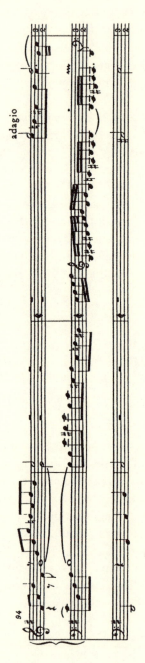

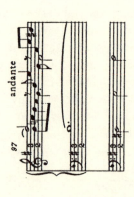

EXAMPLE 4-8. "Allein Gott in der Höh sei Ehr," BWV 663a, as printed in the *Neue Bach-Ausgabe.* Bärenreiter-Verlag, Kassel. Reprinted by permission.

this symbol or printed it as a brace that indicates both notes are to be played by the right hand. But arpeggiation here, and on the next beat as well, makes for a nice violinistic effect (which could also be used for the three-voice manual chords in m. 105).

The score of this work also happens to contain between its two versions more verbal instructions than any other setting in the Great Eighteen. Both versions are headed "Cantabile," a word that literally means "songlike" and that implies a legato touch. The next verbal instruction in either version is "adagio," which occurs at the end of the left-hand cadenza found toward the end of the piece (see Example 4-8). During this cadenza, for the only time in the work, the steady eighth-note surface motion begun in the first bar gives way to a barrage of sixteenths and thirty-seconds. Three beats later, as the eighth notes return, the word "andante" appears in both manuscript sources for the early version. No further verbal instructions of any kind are present in either version.

The obvious conclusions to be drawn are (1) that andante is the tempo for the entire piece, save the cadenza; (2) that Bach is associating *cantabile* with a moderate tempo; and (3) that he merely forgot to write "andante" after the cadenza in the revised version. To judge from Marshall's research, an appropriate metronome setting would be $\downarrow = 60$.

Concerning Bach's use of the term "cantabile," there is reason to believe he is using the locution here for the first time and that he learned it through his study of Vivaldi's concertos. As Marshall points out, the word's earliest appearance in a Bach autograph is from 1721 (in the fifth Brandenburg Concerto), and we have no evidence that he knew of it until 1712–14, when he appears to have composed this organ chorale. One of Vivaldi's concertos transcribed for organ by Bach (BWV 593) also employs this word three times.[50] As discussed in chapter 1, he evidently got to know Vivaldi's music—and this concerto in particular—in 1713.

To return to the matter of tempo, these tempo markings should not be taken at face value. For one thing, a ritard is definitely in order slightly before the "adagio" marking. Likewise, once the "adagio" marking has been reached, the music should continue to slow gradually until the return of the eighth notes on the downbeat of the next bar. Obviously, the "andante" inscription in the early version appears a beat too late in both of its sources (and, consequently, in the *Neue Bach-Ausgabe* as well).

Of course, anyone with musical sense will arrive at these same conclusions on his or her own. Editors have been making these recommendations ever since Mendelssohn did so in 1846, and this is basically how most performers approach the work today. To judge from how he annotated his copy of the Peters edition, this is also how Arnold Schoenberg felt the piece should be played.[51]

"ALLEIN GOTT IN DER HÖH SEI EHR" (ALONE TO GOD ON HIGH BE HONOR), BWV 664

Autograph Heading: *Trio sup[er] / Allein Gott / in der Höh / seÿ Ehr. / a 2 Clav et / Ped. di J. S. Bach*

The "Allein Gott" trilogy concludes with possibly the most popular chorale trio ever written, one likewise characterized by fast perpetual motion in the rhythm (sixteenth notes) one-fourth the value of the main pulse. Indeed, in terms of its "brilliance and ease of writing" this scintillating work has been compared favorably to Bach's trio sonatas for organ.[52] Written in the sharp-laden key of A major, here is a test of coordination and dexterity (and stamina) for any player. The piece was required for the first round of the 1998–2000 AGO National Young Artists Competition in Organ Performance.

As discussed in chapter 1, Bach follows the same unorthodox plan as in the trio on "Herr Jesu Christ": a free trio in ritornello form joined to a cantus firmus chorale. But as Werner Breig has discussed, these two works also differ on some rather fundamental points.[53] For one thing, the two episodes within the "Allein Gott" trio, each of which is stated twice, are significantly longer and more thematically independent of the ritornello; they also incline toward homorhythmic texture in the upper parts. Remarkably, the first episode features violinistic broken chords and a stepwise series of long trills (which are usually performed without any break whatever). Similar episodic material appears in the first movement of Bach's G-major trio sonata for organ.

The "Allein Gott" trio is also over twenty bars longer than "Herr Jesu Christ," even though only the first two phrases of the chorale tune appear in its cantus firmus section. Thus, the free trio comprises a far greater percentage of the overall work, seven-eighths, to be exact (as compared to about one-third in "Herr Jesu Christ"). But despite this statistic, the chorale tune is still integrated into the overall work to a far greater extent, since the ritornello paraphrases all the notes of the first phrase, rather than just half.

A final discrepancy is the basic form used, for while "Herr Jesu Christ" amounts to a loose binary structure (as the preceding description would imply), the "Allein Gott" trio contains three independent sections, each of which has a particular function. The piece opens with six fugal statements of the ritornello, all in the major mode, and with the first episode postponed all the way to measure 35. But once this episode begins, virtually nothing *but* episodes occur for the next forty-five bars; only two ritornello statements are to be found, and for the first and only times in the piece they are in the minor mode (mm. 44–46 and 65–67). These two contrasting sections (mm. 1–34 and 35–79) comprise the first two parts of the form.

To conclude, Bach writes a third, smaller section in which the first two chorale phrases proper are stated *pedaliter*. This section begins, however, with two fugal statements of the ritornello in measures 80–85 that are in essence a note-for-note restatement of the work's first five bars. Combined with the pedal statement of the first phrase of the hymn tune in measures 85–87, these two fugal statements serve as a reprise of the three in measures 1–12. Both passages commence with a right-hand statement in the tonic (with the countersubject in the left hand), followed by a left-hand statement in the dominant (with the counter-subject in the right hand), followed by a pedal statement back in the tonic. The sense of return is strong enough to suggest an ABA scheme, along the lines of an abbreviated da capo aria.

"JESUS CHRISTUS, UNSER HEILAND" (JESUS CHRIST, OUR SAVIOR), BWV 665

Autograph heading: *Jesus Christus unser Heyland. sub Comunione. pedaliter di J. S. Bach.*

This hymn, whose first two lines read: "Jesus Christus, unser Heiland, der von uns den Gotteszorn wandt" ("Jesus Christ, our Savior, who turned God's wrath away from us"), should not be confused with the Easter chorale "Jesus Christus, unser Heiland, der den Tod überwand" set by Bach in the *Orgelbüchlein*. Like "Schmücke dich," its text represents an impassioned commentary on the Lord's Supper. That Bach thought of the chorale in a eucharistic context is attested to by the label *sub Comunione* found in the work heading.

No doubt one of the most appealing aspects of the work is word painting, for here different countermelodies depict successive lines of the text's first stanza. As Spitta first observed, at the onset of the third line ("Through his bitter suffering") the chorale tune is paired with a descending chromatic scale.[54] For the fourth and final line ("Saved us from the pain of hell"), rising thirty-second notes suddenly appear, as the mood shifts dramatically from gloom to joy. Bach accentuates this dichotomy by saving for last the most emphatic statement of the chromatic figure, that in parallel thirds and sixths. Also noteworthy is his tendency toward consecutive statements of the thirty-second-note motive, especially the three statements in measure 44, where the hands twice trade off on repeated notes.

In the realm of purely musical matters, one realizes soon enough that *four* different countermelodies are at work in this composition, one for each of the four chorale phrases. While this procedure leads to fragmentation, all the phrases are nonetheless presented in the same voice order (tenor–alto–bass–soprano) and key sequence (tonic–dominant–tonic–tonic).[55] The only difference is that the pedals drop out immediately after stating each of the first two phrases. The bass voice continues, but in the left hand and of course with the same registration as all the other voices. Thus, the soprano statements lack the bold, distinctive underscoring that pedal stops could provide.

Bach rectifies this problem later in the work by maintaining the pedal line to the very end of each section, even if this means nothing more than adding a pedal point (as in mm. 35–38). In this regard, his handling of the final phrase is especially impressive, as the pedal line there lasts nine full bars, commencing with the chorale phrase (mm. 44–46), continuing with freely composed scalar figuration (mm. 46–49), and ending with a mighty double pedal point. Simultaneously, the texture thickens from three all the way to eight voices.

The inscription *in pleno Organo* found in Walther's copy of the early version may or may not be authentic, but there is no better registration. Within these confines, the player should feel free to add stops between sections. This poses difficulties only on the downbeat of measure 38, where the final statement of the chromatic scale merges in the same chord with the first note (d′) of the last phrase. If the registration is increased after this chord, any break before the e′ quarter note should be minimal, so as not to suggest that the phrase begins there.

"JESUS CHRISTUS, UNSER HEILAND" (JESUS CHRIST, OUR SAVIOR), BWV 666

Heading inscribed by J. C. Altnikol: *Jesus Christus unser p. /*
alio modo / di / J. S. Bach[56]

This second setting of "Jesus Christus" may be regarded as the only *manualiter* work in the Great Eighteen, but it does conclude with a tonic pedal point. In this respect, the piece recalls certain youthful keyboard fugues by Bach such as the Fugues in C Major and A Major, BWV 946 and 949, and the Fugue in A Major on a Theme by Albinoni,

EXAMPLE 4-9. "Jesus Christus, unser Heiland," BWV 666a, as edited by Heinz Lohmann, Edition Breitkopf 6587. Breitkopf & Härtel, Wiesbaden—Leipzig. Used by permission.

BWV 950. Another indicator of an early date is the cadenza-like interlude used between the first three phrases, for such solo figuration is a trademark of Bach's "Arnstadt Congregational Chorales." Here, however, the material becomes woven into the contrapuntal fabric for the remainder of the composition.

As Peter Williams has discussed, the early version gives two extra instructions to the player: to phrase the opening motive as ♩♩ ♩ and to alternate hands during the arpeggiated figuration at measures 35–36 (see Example 4-9).[57] The six-note motive at the heart of this passage appears four times earlier in the piece (m. 26, beats 4–6; m. 28, beats 10–12; m. 31, beats 4–6; and m. 33, beats 10–12), but in the early version with a descending triad from the third to the fifth notes, followed by an ascending third. In the revised version, all four statements conform to the contour used in measures 35–36. Thus, the revised version enjoys a greater degree of motivic unity.

"KOMM, GOTT SCHÖPFER, HEILIGER GEIST" (COME, GOD CREATOR, HOLY GHOST), BWV 667

Heading inscribed by J. C. Altnikol: *Kom Gott Schöpfer Heiliger Geist. in Organo pleno con Pedale / obigato* [sic] *d[i] J. S. Bach*

The two variations of this work may well symbolize two different Pentecost themes. In the first, pedal notes normally sound on the third eighth note of the beat, as if to depict the third member of the Holy Trinity. In the second, fast sixteenth notes in scalar motion run through every bar, like a giant gust of wind.

As mentioned in chapter 1, Bach crafted this piece by taking the early version of the *Orgelbüchlein* setting of this hymn (mm. 1–8) and

EXAMPLE 4-10. "Komm, Gott Schöpfer, Heiliger Geist," BWV 667

coupling it to one newly composed (mm. 13–26). Many writers have frowned on this structure as "arbitrary,"[58] because the two variations are based largely on different accompanimental figuration. But is this not how any chorale partita operates? Besides, the figuration of the second variation is clearly anticipated in the first, beginning in measures 4 and 6. Measures 7–8 then adopt steady motion in scalar sixteenths, as does the bridge between variations (mm. 9–12). This common material creates a smooth transition between variations and imparts a sense of organic unity to the overall work. The effect is also that of a gradual acceleration.

The sheer energy of this piece—which is only heightened by Altnikol's instruction of *Organo pleno*—manifests itself in other ways as well. If played fast enough, its compound meter easily suggests a gigue, especially in Variation 1, which features regular two-bar phrases. Furthermore, the syncopated pedal line of this variation is almost primitively dancelike in nature. Most impressive are the last two measures, where the music suddenly veers to the minor subdominant and—in an outburst of chromaticism—spells the composer's name (see Example 4-10).

The sources preserve three different versions. The earliest, known as BWV 667b, differs from the final version primarily in its paucity of sixteenth notes in Variation 1 (eighth notes are used instead) and its inclusion of parallel octaves and clumsy dissonances in Variation 2.[59] In the intermediary version, BWV 667a, these infelicities are purged.

"VOR DEINEN THRON TRET ICH HIERMIT" (BEFORE YOUR THRONE I NOW APPEAR), BWV 668

Heading inscribed by anonymous copyist: *Vor deinen Thron tret ich pp*[60]

As discussed in chapter 2, this work—Bach's "deathbed" chorale—is a revised version of "Wenn wir in höchsten Nöten sein," BWV 668a, a complete composition of forty-five bars. "Vor deinen Thron," conversely, is a mere fragment that breaks off in the middle of measure 26. In comparing the first twenty-six measures of these two works, one sees that two of Bach's revisions again have to do with rhythmic sharpening. In both instances (m. 9, bass; m. 26, soprano), pairs of eighth notes were altered to dotted eighths followed by sixteenths, resulting in greater rhythmic variety and a more polyphonic texture. The change to the bass voice in measure 9 also allows for motivic interplay with the soprano.

Only two other changes were made. First, in the tenor voice of measure 7 ♪♪♪ figures replace quarter notes, more or less in accordance with the alto. But the most substantial revision occurs in the bass voice of measure 10, where, on the third beat, E replaces G. This means the difference between a G-major and E-minor chord and, more important, between an authentic and deceptive cadence.

We can only guess about Bach's revisions—if he made any at all—from measure 27 on. Unfortunately, this section of "Wenn wir" contains no passages directly analogous to those revised in the first twenty-six bars, so any attempt to revise it "as Bach might have" is doomed to futility. The performer must simply be content with playing the first twenty-six bars as they appear in "Vor deinen Thron" and the remaining measures as found in "Wenn wir." Most editions also print the work in this composite form.

The original sources indicate neither two manuals nor pedal, but this is how the work is traditionally played (with, of course, the soprano voice on its own manual). Performing on one manual is no problem, because the soprano and alto never cross. But playing *manualiter* is difficult at best, due to several awkward reaches, the hardest of which involve ninths and tenths between the bass and tenor in measures 9–10.

Last but not least, questions have been raised about the suitability of the chorale "Vor deinen Thron" as a deathbed text. For although it was sometimes sung to the tune of "Wenn wir," the text was customarily designated not as a "Death and Dying" hymn but as one appropriate merely for "Morning, Midday, or Evening." In essence, the chorale summarizes the Christian faith. More than one commentator has argued that only the last of its fifteen stanzas refers explicitly to dying and judgment.[61]

Still, the opening line of this hymn unmistakably alludes to the subject of death, and perhaps Bach placed no significance whatever on how the text continues. The original title, of course, bears similar implications, but it makes its plea from the perspective of a corporate body: "Wenn *wir* in höchsten Nöten sein." "Vor deinen Thron tret *ich* hiermit" is the testimony of an individual.

Chapter 5

RECEPTION HISTORY

To conclude, we will study the "reception" of the Great Eighteen chorales. In a musicological context, the term "reception history" implies the study of compositions as mirrored in the reactions of critics, artists, and audiences. But a work's historical reception may also be chronicled in sources devoid of aesthetic content. Take, for instance, the over forty extant manuscript copies of the Great Eighteen from the eighteenth and early nineteenth centuries.[1] In no case do these sources tell us anything in particular about the scribe's attitude toward the music. Yet their number alone indicates that the works have been relatively popular since their inception.

For most of these sources, furthermore, something is known about the scribe's identity or the manuscript's provenance. This information signifies when and where the collection began to achieve its popularity and how it figured in musical life of the day. Not surprisingly, most of the scribes who can be identified were church organists who also composed organ music and had private organ pupils. Thus, the Great Eighteen served these individuals as music they could play at worship services, as compositional models for their own organ chorales, and as pedagogical material.

In this chapter, then, "reception history" will be interpreted in the broadest sense of the term, encompassing any evidence that bears on how the Great Eighteen have been received over the years. Accordingly, we will examine, in addition to aesthetic responses, such themes as the collection's dissemination in manuscript and printed form, its use as a model for transcriptions, its performance history, and its influence on composers.

THE EIGHTEENTH CENTURY

The reception of the Great Eighteen is remarkably similar to that of Bach's other large manuscript collection of organ chorales, the *Orgel-büchlein*.[2] It starts with Bach himself, simply because his private students and colleagues prepared copies of the chorales. These students and colleagues, in turn, transmitted the music to *their* students and colleagues, and so forth. To cite just one example, a copy of "Schmücke dich" in the hand of Bach's pupil Johann Christian Kittel was clearly the source from which Kittel's pupils J. A. Dröbs and J. N. Gebhardi made their copies.

To what degree did Bach teach the Great Eighteen? The relative paucity of extant student copies implies that he did not teach them as regularly as such collections as the Inventions and Sinfonias or the *Well-Tempered Clavier*, both of which are explicitly didactic.[3] Yet he obviously taught the pieces over many years' time, if only intermittently, for most of the student copies that have survived are by students from various periods of the composer's life, made during the period of instruction.

These students include J. T. Krebs, who studied under Bach in Weimar from 1714 to 1717 and left behind copies of fourteen of the chorales; H. N. Gerber, who was a Bach pupil in Leipzig around 1725 and whose copy of the first "Allein Gott" setting is extant; and J. F. Agricola, who studied with Bach in Leipzig from 1738 to 1741, during which time he copied out the two arrangements of "Jesus Christus, unser Heiland."[4] (The aforementioned copy of "Schmücke dich" by Bach's pupil Kittel, which is lost, dates presumably from very late in Bach's life, as Kittel studied with Bach between 1748 and 1750.)

Another student copy to survive is that by Johann Caspar Vogler of the third setting of "Allein Gott."[5] Bach taught Vogler in Weimar from 1710 to 1715 (and in Arnstadt around 1706), but this manuscript appears to have originated sometime after 1730. Nevertheless, it shows that the Great Eighteen continued to circulate in Weimar—where Vogler was court organist from 1721 until his death in 1763—years after Bach's departure in 1717. It also suggests that Vogler had studied this work with Bach in Weimar and prepared this copy to replace one he had made during the period of study.

We must also consider Johann Ludwig Krebs, who studied with Bach in the late 1720s and early 1730s. Of Bach's pupils, Krebs was the most prolific as a composer of organ music, and he often relied on his teacher's works as models. Two of Krebs's organ chorales are obviously based on pieces from the Great Eighteen.[6] He probably studied these works with Bach (and prepared copies of them at Bach's request) or gained access to them through his father J. T. Krebs, whose manuscript copies of both pieces survive.

As Examples 5-1 and 5-2 show, Krebs's setting of "Jesu, meines Lebens Leben" begins exactly like the first arrangement of "Nun komm" from the Great Eighteen, with a walking-bass pedal line in eighth notes that moves stepwise from G to the sixth degree of the scale; with pre-imitation in quarter notes of the opening chorale phrase, first in the tenor on g and then in the alto on d′; and with the same three-note motive (♪ ♩♪) in the inner voices. The model for Krebs's trio on "Herr Jesu Christ, dich zu uns wend" is the Great Eighteen setting of the same chorale (see Examples 5-3 and 5-4). Indeed, two of the sources for Krebs's work name Bach as the composer. Both pieces begin as "free" chorale trios in ritornello form, with the same triadic eighth-note motive, but end with the entire hymn tune played in the pedals, mostly in quarter notes, in the manner of a cantus firmus chorale.

Except for Agricola, who settled in Berlin, all these pupils remained in central Germany. Other figures who contributed to the dissemination of the Great Eighteen in this region were J. G. Walther, organist of the Weimar town church, and the Weimar-area organists J. N. Mempell (1713–47) and J. G. Preller (1717–85). Walther's copies of nine works from the collection survive, and a dozen different pieces are preserved in a manuscript assembled in the 1730s and 1740s by Mempell and Preller.[7] In addition to being colleagues in Weimar for nine years, Bach

EXAMPLE 5-1. "Nun komm, der Heiden Heiland," BWV 659

EXAMPLE 5-2. Johann Ludwig Krebs, "Jesu, meines Lebens Leben"

EXAMPLE 5-3. "Herr Jesu Christ, dich zu uns wend," BWV 655

and Walther were second cousins. Although there is no proof that Mempell or Preller knew Bach personally, they obviously had close ties to the Bach circle. Mempell may have been a pupil of the Gräfenroda organist J. P. Kellner, a personal acquaintance of Bach's and perhaps one of his pupils as well; Preller may have studied under J. T. Krebs.

After Bach's death, the Great Eighteen continued to circulate in and around the city of Leipzig. Thirteen of them were among the 114 Bach

EXAMPLE 5-4. Johann Ludwig Krebs, "Herr Jesu Christ, dich zu uns wend"

organ chorales owned in manuscript form by the Leipzig publishing house of Breitkopf. This firm possessed literally thousands of eighteenth-century music manuscripts for the purpose of selling handwritten copies of music, and it regularly advertised its stock through cataloges. Once a work had been ordered, it was copied anew by a Breitkopf scribe from one of the firm's "house" manuscripts. The newly created manuscript or "sale" copy was then sold to the customer.

The Breitkopf house manuscripts of these 114 organ chorales have not survived. But these lost sources, which were completed by 1764, appear to have been used by the Bach devotee C. F. Penzel (1737–1801) in preparing a manuscript that contains eleven of the Great Eighteen chorales.[8] According to the inscription "Leipzig, 22 January 1766," this manuscript originated about ten months before Penzel became cantor in nearby Merseburg (a post he retained until his death). Three sale copies of Breitkopf's collection of Bach organ chorales are extant. One of these was purchased by the alleged Bach pupil J. C. Oley, organist in Aschersleben from 1762 until his death in 1789. Oley's copy preserves seven of the Great Eighteen.

Looking northward, one finds that the theorist J. P. Kirnberger (1721–83) was largely responsible for the transmission of the music in and around Berlin during the second half of the eighteenth century. Upon his appointment in 1758 to the court of Princess Anna Amalia of Prussia, he oversaw the preparation of a voluminous collection of Bach manuscripts.[9] All but two of the Great Eighteen chorales (the two settings of "Jesus Christus, unser Heiland") are contained in these sources. Kirnberger could have gained access to the works through his Berlin colleague C. P. E. Bach, who came into possession of the autograph manuscript sometime after his father's death in 1750. By the same token, though, Kirnberger had been one of Sebastian Bach's pupils around 1740 and might have prepared copies of the pieces at that time, from which the scribes under his supervision could have made their copies.

Meanwhile, many of Bach's organ works were also being disseminated in southern Germany by the Nuremberg organist Leonard Scholz (1720–98). Scholz, though, often copied the music in abbreviated and simplified form, presumably to compensate for his relatively weak performing technique. No fewer than five such versions of the Great Eighteen setting of "Herr Jesu Christ" are found among Scholz's Bach copies, only one of which is listed (as BWV 655b) in the *Bach-Werke-Verzeichnis.*[10]

As Table 5-1 illustrates, Scholz retains in all five versions the concluding pedal statement of the hymn tune. But he drastically abridges the preceding material, which features a far more active pedal part.[11] Indeed, the three Scholz versions in F major avoid the pedals altogether until the statement of the chorale melody. (His reasons for transposing the work are unclear.)

As Example 5-5 shows, these three versions also involve a variant form of Bach's ritornello theme (which appears unchanged in Scholz version #2). Although Scholz preserves the general contour of the mel-

TABLE 5-1 Versions of "Herr Jesu Christ, dich zu uns wend," BWV 655

Version	Key, Number of Measures	Chorale Tune Stated in Pedals
BWV 655 (autograph version)	G major, 73 mm.	from m. 52
BWV 655a (Bach's early version)	G major, 73 mm.	from m. 52
BWV 655b (Scholz version #1)	G major, 29 mm.	from m. 8
BWV 655c	G major, 29 mm.	(no statement)
Scholz version #2	G major, 31 mm.	from m. 10
Scholz version #3	F major, 39 mm.	from m. 11
Scholz version #4	F major, 39 mm.	from m. 11
Scholz version #5	F major, 22 mm.	from m. 4

ody, he concludes with a syncopated octave leap. Such a discrepancy suggests that he made certain alterations for purely artistic reasons, however misguided. (Observe his completely different rewrite of the ritornello in BWV 655b.) This syncopated idea seems too close to that used in BWV 655c for there not to be a connection, but the nature of that connection remains obscure. Ironically, BWV 655c is the only version in which the hymn tune is not presented in the pedals.

THE NINETEENTH CENTURY

By the turn of the nineteenth century, the Great Eighteen were known throughout Germany, though almost entirely in manuscript form. The only chorale available in print was the early version of "Vor deinen Thron," first published in 1751 under the title "Wenn wir in höchsten Nöten sein" as a supplement to Bach's *Art of Fugue*. Because of its association with this opus and, of course, its legendary status as the composer's deathbed chorale, this work has always been popular. By 1845, two years before the Great Eighteen were first published complete, six different prints of this chorale had been issued (see Table 5-2).[12] We should not be surprised, either, that the earliest known aesthetic response to any of the Great Eighteen chorales was directed at this piece. It comes from the theologian Johann Michael Schmidt, who in 1754 hailed "Wenn wir" as nothing less than an antidote to materialism.[13]

Only three other works from the collection were published prior to Felix Mendelssohn's edition of fourteen of them in 1846, although the Swiss publisher Hans Georg Nägeli (1773–1836) had evidently conceived of a complete edition well before this date.[14] The first to appear

BWV 655 (autograph version)

BWV 655a (Bach's early version)

BWV 655b (Scholz version #1)

BWV 655c

Scholz version #2

EXAMPLE 5-5. Versions of "Herr Jesu Christ, dich zu uns wend," BWV 655

114

Scholz version #3

Scholz version #4

Scholz version #5

EXAMPLE 5-5. *Continued*

was the third setting of "Allein Gott," which was included in J. G. Schicht's four-volume anthology, *J. S. Bach's Choral-Vorspiele für die Orgel* (1803–6). This publication, which contains a total of thirty-eight works, represents the first collected edition of Bach's organ chorales, and it introduced many a musician to this incomparable repertory.

One of these was Robert Schumann, who throughout his life was a passionate advocate for Bach's music. As Schumann's diaries make clear, during 1837 and 1838 he diligently studied Schicht's print.[15] We know nothing of Schumann's reception of the "Allein Gott" setting in particular, and this is only one of many trios found in this anthology. But Schumann allegedly played Bach organ trios at the piano (perhaps a pedal piano?), thereby developing a left hand that could negotiate fast, disjunct passages with great accuracy.[16] Hence, this arrangement of "Allein Gott" may have played a role in Schumann's development as a pianist. One wonders if there is any connection between these left-hand organ-trio exercises and Schumann's notorious injury to his right hand in 1832. Did he hope to strengthen his left hand to the point of compensating for its crippled partner? Whatever the case, according to one of Schumann's diary entries from 1837, he "played through" Schicht's anthology in addition to studying it in the academic sense.[17]

TABLE 5-2 The Publication History of the Great Eighteen Chorales to 1847

Title of Publication	Editor (or Author of Treatise)	Date and Place of Publication	Title and BWV No. of Chorale(s) Published
Die Kunst der Fuge	probably C. P. E. Bach	1751, Leipzig	"Wenn wir in höchsten Nöten sein," BWV 668a
J. S. Bach's Choral-Vorspiele für die Orgel, vol. 2	J. G. Schicht	1803, Leipzig	"Allein Gott in der Höh sei Ehr," BWV 664b
Practische Orgelschule	F. W. Schütze	1838, Dresden	"Wenn wir in höchsten Nöten sein," BWV 668a
Sammlung der besten Meisterwerke des 17. und 18. Jahrhunderts für die Orgel	Franz Commer	1839, Berlin	"Wenn wir in höchsten Nöten sein," BWV 668a
Der Orgelfreund, vol. 4, no. 5	G. W. Körner and A. G. Ritter	1842, Erfurt	"Wenn wir in höchsten Nöten sein," BWV 668a
Joh. Seb. Bach's vierstimmige Kirchengesänge	K. F. Becker	1843, Leipzig	"Wenn wir in höchsten Nöten sein," BWV 668a
Caecilia, eine Zeitschrift für die musikalische Welt, vol. 23, no. 89	S. W. Dehn	1844, Mainz	"Schmücke dich, o liebe Seele," BWV 654; "Nun komm, der Heiden Heiland," BWV 659
Die Kunst des Orgelspiels	A. G. Ritter	1844, Erfurt	"Schmücke dich, o liebe Seele," BWV 654
Caecilia: Tonstücke für die Orgel, vol. 1, no. 2	K. F. Becker	1845, Leipzig	"Wenn wir in höchsten Nöten sein," BWV 668a
John Sebastian Bach's Organ Compositions on Corales (Psalm Tunes), books 3 and 4	Felix Mendelssohn	1846, London	all the chorales except BWV 664, 665, 666, and 668

Title of Publication	Editor (or Author of Treatise)	Date and Place of Publication	Title and BWV No. of Chorale(s) Published
15 Grosse Choral-Vorspiele für die Orgel von Johann Sebastian Bach	Felix Mendelssohn	1846, Leipzig	all the chorales except BWV 664, 665, 666, and 668
Johann Sebastian Bach's Komposi-tionen für die Orgel, vols. 6 and 7	F. C. Griepenkerl and Ferdinand Roitzsch	1847, Leipzig	complete collection

The other two works published prior to Mendelssohn's edition, "Schmücke dich" and the first setting of "Nun komm," have long been favorites. Perhaps they were not universally held in such high esteem as early as 1844, the date of their first editions. Nonetheless, one of these editors (A. G. Ritter) acclaimed "Schmücke dich" one of Bach's "most intimate and lovely" compositions and praised its solo soprano line as "beautifully decorated yet free of any gaudiness."[18]

Another nineteenth-century musician with a special fondness for this chorale was Felix Mendelssohn, the most ardent Bach champion of his era. In fact, "Schmücke dich" was reportedly Mendelssohn's favorite piece of music, probably because of the same attributes discussed in chapter 4: an unusually lyrical chorale tune, sweet accompanimental writing in parallel thirds and sixths, beautiful ornamental figuration, and an overall mystical quality consistent with the ritual of communion.

We learn initially of Mendelssohn's enthusiasm for the work from two letters written at the age of twenty-two to his parents and siblings. The first, written in Lindau on September 5, 1831, merely includes the sentence: "I found [here yesterday] evening a wonderful organ, where I could play *Schmücke dich, o liebe Seele* to my heart's content."[19] But in the second letter, written about a month later in Munich, Mendelssohn explained not only his emotional reaction to the piece but also how he performed it. He offered these comments in particular to his sister and fellow Bach enthusiast Fanny:

> I also play the organ every day for an hour. But unfortunately I cannot practice as I wish because the pedal lacks the five uppermost notes. Thus, I cannot play any of Sebastian Bach's music on it. But

the stops are wonderfully beautiful, especially for chorale settings. The heavenly, liquid tone of the instrument is edifying. In particular, Fanny, I have here discovered the stops that ought to be used in playing Sebastian Bach's *Schmücke dich, o liebe Seele*. They seem actually made for this piece and sound so touching that I am invariably awestruck when I begin to play it. For the moving parts I have an eight-foot flute, and also a very soft four-foot flute, which continuously floats above the chorale tune. You know this effect from Berlin. But here there is a keyboard with reed stops on which I can play the chorale tune, so I use a mellow oboe, a very soft four-foot clarion, and a viola. This renders the chorale tune so subdued and glowing, it is as if distant human voices are singing from the depths of the heart.[20]

To fully appreciate these two excerpts, consider Mendelssohn's activities around 1830 and his prior knowledge of Bach's organ music. Both letters date from Mendelssohn's *Bildungsreise* of 1830–32, a series of trips throughout Europe undertaken (at the urging of his parents) for the sake of his general education. During these sojourns, the young artist played all manner of concerts, kept busy as a composer, and made the acquaintance of numerous important musicians. He also made it a priority to continue practicing the organ, with special emphasis on Bach. As Mendelssohn put it himself, in a letter to his family of September 30, 1831: "Today, I played [the organ] the entire morning. I have also begun to study the instrument seriously, because it is actually a shame that I cannot play Sebastian Bach's major works."[21] His fascination with "Schmücke dich," then, represents just one example of his intensive study of Bach's organ music at this time.

How did Mendelssohn first come to know the work? Quite possibly at the hands of the Berlin organist August Wilhelm Bach, who had been Mendelssohn's organ teacher in 1820–21. August Wilhelm specialized in the organ music of J. S. Bach—although these two Bachs were not related—and taught this repertory to the young Mendelssohn.[22] That Felix played "Schmücke dich" while growing up in Berlin is strongly suggested by his remark to Fanny that she had heard "this effect" in Berlin, which seems to refer less to flute stops in general than to this organ chorale in particular. Fanny, who is known to have accompanied Felix to his organ lessons,[23] may even have been present when her brother played "Schmücke dich" for his teacher.

In conjunction with his appointment as conductor of the Gewandhaus Orchestra, Mendelssohn moved to Leipzig in the summer of 1835, and he found there a new friend in Robert Schumann. Such was Schumann's admiration for his new colleague that he immediately inducted Mendelssohn into his imaginary Davidsbund (League of David) under the sobriquet "Felix Meritis." Early on in their friendship, Mendelssohn must have played "Schmücke dich" in Schumann's presence, for in 1836, after searching unsuccessfully for Bach's grave, Schumann wrote in his periodical, the *Neue Zeitschrift für Musik*:

> I prefer to picture [Bach] seated upright at his organ in the prime of his life, the music swelling out from under his feet and fingers, the congregation looking up at him raptly, and possibly a few angels among them.
>
> You, Felix Meritis, a man of equally superior intellect and character, played one of his chorale preludes on that organ; the text was "Schmücke dich, o liebe Seele." The *cantus firmus* was hung with wreaths of gilded leaves, and flooded with a beatitude that prompted you to confess: "If life were to deprive me of hope and faith, this single chorale would replenish me with both."[24]

This famous excerpt reveals the full (and truly remarkable) extent of Mendelssohn's affection for this chorale. It also tells us what particularly impressed Schumann about the work: the exquisite ornamentation of the chorale tune—perhaps in the ritornello as well as throughout the solo soprano line—and its "spiritual" quality. Schumann's reference to "that organ" strongly suggests that the performance took place at St. Thomas, where Bach had been cantor.

This church also provides the locale of the next chapter in our story, in which Schumann makes another appearance. For on August 6, 1840, Mendelssohn played an all-Bach organ recital at St. Thomas (to raise funds for a monument to the composer), and the second piece on the program was "Schmücke dich." In his glowing review of the concert, Schumann ventured that the work was "as priceless, deep, and full of soul as any piece of music that ever sprang from a true artist's imagination."[25]

In the same review, Schumann also noted correctly that "Schmücke dich" was at that time still unpublished. Four years later, though, two different editions had appeared, and Mendelssohn followed in 1846 with one of his own, a copy of which he gave to Schumann in October of that year.[26] Mendelssohn's edition contains thirteen other works from the Great Eighteen.

A final bit of documentation that bears on Mendelssohn and his favorite organ chorale involves the historian Johann Gustav Droysen, another close acquaintance of the composer.[27] In March of 1847, Droysen's wife passed away, leaving him in utter despair. Writing to him a month later, Mendelssohn offered various remedies for his friend's melancholy, one of which was a performance of "Schmücke dich": "If music brings you joy, you could have your local organist play you

'Schmücke dich, o liebe Seele' by Sebastian Bach!"[28] Obviously, Mendelssohn was hoping the piece would have the same cathartic effect on Droysen that he had discussed with Schumann.

We do not know if Droysen heeded his friend's advice. His response the following month, though, implies that he would have been more than receptive to the work:

> You say you would like "Schmücke dich, o liebe Seele" played for me. When I was in Berlin last year, Fanny invited me to a musicale. "The Lord's Time Is the Best Time" was sung—and I knew immediately what I was in store for! Now that was a sermon![29]

Droysen is alluding here to the tradition of Sunday musicales at the home of Felix and Fanny's parents. Bach was regular fare at these events, and there is good reason to believe that Droysen is referring to one of that composer's most beloved church cantatas. First of all, the fact that "Schmücke dich" is a Bach work suggests that "The Lord's Time" is also; otherwise, Droysen's mention of the Berlin concert is a non sequitur. Perhaps he was anticipating that "Schmücke dich" might be just as edifying as that vocal composition, which he identifies as "Des Herren Zeit ist die beste Zeit." The title of Bach's Cantata 106 is virtually the same: *Gottes Zeit ist die allerbeste Zeit.* Most important, we know that Fanny led a performance of this profoundly theological work—hence the sermon metaphor—at one of the musicales in 1835.[30] Furthermore, Felix had conducted the piece in public on more than one occasion, and he intended one of these performances as a requiem—the work was undoubtedly written for a funeral service—for his father, who had responded most enthusiastically to Fanny's performance.[31] The cantata was obviously a family favorite.

As for Mendelssohn's edition of the Great Eighteen, it belongs to his four-volume set, *John Sebastian Bach's Organ Compositions on Corales (Psalm Tunes).*[32] The series was first published in London by Coventry & Hollier, but each volume was almost immediately reprinted in Leipzig by Breitkopf & Härtel. Volumes 1 and 2, which contain most of the *Orgelbüchlein*, appeared in 1845 under the title *44 Short Organ Preludes on Corales.* Volumes 3 and 4, which contain most of the Great Eighteen chorales, appeared the following year under the title *15 Grand Preludes on Corales.* The two pairs of volumes were clearly meant to complement each other.

Mendelssohn attached a preface to each pair of volumes, but that of the *15 Grand Preludes* is especially interesting in the realm of performance practice. As translated by his friend Karl Klingemann, it reads:

The present 15 Grand Preludes on Corales (as I already observed in my Preface introducing the 44 short Organ Preludes on Corales) are published from several old written copies, nearly concordant amongst themselves, and without any modern addition as to Time, Selection of Stops, or similar matter.

With regard to the Selection of Stops, it might not be superfluous to remark in general that, for the present compositions, the superscription "Full Organ" does not always mean *all* the real Stops of an Organ; furthermore, that whenever the superscription says "for two rows of Keys and Pedal," only soft Stops ought to be used.

In the Prelude No. 6, on the Corale "Oh Lamb of God," it appears necessary to change the Stops at the beginning of each new Verse, so that the third Verse is played with the greatest number of Stops (perhaps towards the end with the full Organ). In No. 2 also, "Come holy Ghost," I would recommend here and there to change the Stops after the termination of the different periods of the Cantus firmus, or gradually to increase the power of the Organ to the end. In No. 3, "On the rivers of Babylon," most probably only an 8 feet Pedal is meant, without any 16 feet Stops.

It need hardly be mentioned that for the Prelude No. 8, as well as for the one No. 14, no 16 feet Stop whatever must be used in the Pedal.

These remarks progress from the general to the specific. Having explained his *Urtext* editorial style, Mendelssohn warns against a too literal interpretation of *Organo Pleno* and advocates "soft" stops for any piece marked for two manuals. Considering that this was the first collected edition of the Great Eighteen, these instructions were probably not the least bit "superfluous," especially outside Germany. Of course, "soft" needs to be understood not as an absolute concept but as relative to "Full Organ."

Mendelssohn next comments on individual pieces, starting with "O Lamm Gottes." Most players today still follow his suggestion of a variation-by-variation increase in registration. He recommends the same approach for the ornamental setting of "Komm, Heiliger Geist," probably to achieve variety in what is a very long and monotonous work. Still, whereas this sort of buildup works well for a set of three variations, adding stops between all nine phrases of this chorale motet seems most excessive, and it thoroughly fragments the work's structure. Mendelssohn also cautions against sixteen-foot pedal registers in "An Wasserflüssen Babylon" and "Von Gott will ich nicht lassen" (Prelude No. 8). His rationale in the former instance is by no means clear; in the latter, however, it surely has all to do with the unusual tenor range of the pedal line.[33]

Although it does not contain all eighteen chorales, Mendelssohn's edition follows the order of the autograph. Its musical text, though, is rife with errors, in part because Mendelssohn had no access to the autograph manuscript.[34] All eighteen works appeared the next year in volumes 6 and 7 of the Peters edition of Bach's complete organ works, edited by F. C. Griepenkerl and Ferdinand Roitzsch. In terms of musical content, this is a very reliable edition—and one still widely used today, despite its use of C clef—since the editors worked directly from Bach's autograph; it also represents the first publication of many of the early versions. Unfortunately, though, this edition gives no sense of the Great Eighteen as a collection, for the works are printed in alphabetical order, interspersed among almost fifty other chorale settings. Not until the publication of Wilhelm Rust's Bachgesellschaft edition in 1878 was there a complete edition that adopted both the order and musical text of the autograph.

One of the owners of this publication was Johannes Brahms, who, like Schumann and Mendelssohn, was deeply involved with Bach's music his entire life.[35] His initial response to the Great Eighteen is unknown. But about twenty years after the publication of Rust's edition, these chorales apparently inspired Brahms in a most profound way.

We are alluding here to the composer's last work, the Eleven Chorale Preludes, composed in May and June of 1896 and published posthumously as Opus 122.[36] To understand this collection, Brahms's dire personal situation in the spring and summer of 1896 must be taken into account. Since 1890 he had been obsessed with his own mortality, and he drew up his will the following year.[37] Three of his best friends—the surgeon Theodor Billroth, the pianist and conductor Hans von Bülow, and the Bach biographer Philipp Spitta—died in 1894, and his closest friend of all, Clara Schumann (Robert's widow), passed away on May 20, 1896. Later that summer, Brahms was diagnosed with liver cancer, the same disease that had claimed his father. He died less than a year later, at the age of sixty-three.

The pall cast by these events clearly manifests itself in the composer's final two works: the organ chorales and the Four Serious Songs, composed in the spring of 1896. Both are set exclusively to sacred texts, several of which deal with death and dying. Brahms knew his days were numbered, and he was making his final peace with God.

No one has ever questioned that these organ chorales also amount to a final tribute to Bach, the greatest master of the genre. But what Bach works in particular did Brahms take as his models? The traditional answer has been, with regard to form and technique, the *Orgelbüchlein*. Still, the underlying idea for the project seems to come from the Great

Eighteen chorales, or at least the circumstances of their composition as postulated by musicologists of the late nineteenth century.[38]

An amateur Bach scholar himself, Brahms would have read in the preface of Rust's Bachgesellschaft edition that Bach compiled the Great Eighteen in the last year or two of his life. Thus, Brahms's decision to author a collection of organ chorales as he felt his own life slipping away may be seen as an attempt to emulate Bach biographically as well as musically. Both Rust and Brahms's friend Spitta, in his Bach biography of 1873–80, also maintained that the Great Eighteen setting of "Vor deinen Thron" was Bach's "swan song" (as Rust called it), which the blind composer dictated on his deathbed. As discussed in chapter 4, the opening line of this hymn doubtless implies death as its subject matter. The final work in Brahms's collection—the last bit of music he ever wrote—dwells on the same topic. Set to the chorale "O Welt, ich muss dich lassen" (O world, I must leave you), its text depicts death as a prelude to eternal heavenly rest.

Appropriately enough, Brahms also figures in the first published transcription of a chorale from the Great Eighteen, that of "O Lamm Gottes" by his friend the piano virtuoso Carl Tausig, for he is the dedicatee of Tausig's collection of piano transcriptions in which this arrangement appears (see Table 5-3). For the first two variations, Tausig sticks strictly to his model. But in Variation 3, marked *Grandioso e poco più largo*, he turns this Passiontide hymn into an outright pyrotechnical display. Doublings of every sort occur throughout in both hands (along with a steady increase in volume), even in the last thirteen bars, where the surface motion accelerates from quarter notes to eighths.

Two slightly later Bach transcribers—and the most prolific in music history—were Ferruccio Busoni and Max Reger. Within a two-year span (1898–1900), each issued a collection of Bach organ chorales arranged for piano whose stated purpose was to introduce this repertory to the musical public. Most of these chorales come from the Great Eighteen and the *Orgelbüchlein*.

Busoni labels his manner of arranging "chamber style," in distinction to the more virtuosic and free "concert style" of his piano transcriptions of Bach's free instrumental works. (Still, Busoni's rendition of "Komm, Gott Schöpfer" borders on the bombastic.) As a representative example, take his arrangement of the first setting of "Nun komm," which has been recorded by the likes of Dinu Lipatti and Alfred Brendel.[39] Above all, what makes this piece so effective on the piano is the walking-bass pedal line, which, as Busoni realized, is tailor-made for low left-hand octaves. With the left hand so engaged, the right hand is

TABLE 5-3 Transcriptions of the Great Eighteen Chorales, in Chronological Order, according to Publication Date

Transcriber and Instrumentation	Bibliographical Citation	Title and BWV No. of Chorale(s) Transcribed
Carl Tausig (1841–71) (piano)	*Choralvorspiele für die Orgel von Johann Sebastian Bach: Für das Clavier übertragen von Carl Tausig.* Berlin, n.d. (dedicated to Brahms)	"O Lamm Gottes, unschuldig," BWV 656
Ferruccio Busoni (piano)	*Orgelchoralvorspiele von Johann Sebastian Bach: Auf das Pianoforte im Kammerstyl übertragen von Ferruccio Benvenuto Busoni.* 2 vols. Leipzig, 1898.	"Nun komm, der Heiden Heiland," BWV 659; "Jesus Christus, unser Heiland," BWV 665; "Komm, Gott Schöpfer, Heiliger Geist," BWV 667
Max Reger (piano)	*Ausgewählte Choralvorspiele von Joh. Seb. Bach: Für Klavier zu 2 Händen übertragen von Max Reger.* Vienna, 1900.	"Komm, Heiliger Geist, Herre Gott," BWV 651; "An Wasserflüssen Babylon," BWV 653b; "Schmücke dich, o liebe Seele," BWV 654; "Nun danket alle Gott," BWV 657; "Vor deinen Thron tret ich hiermit," BWV 668
Arnold Schoenberg (orchestra)	*Choralvorspiele von Joh. Seb. Bach, instrumentiert von Arnold Schönberg.* Vienna, 1925.	"Schmücke dich, o liebe Seele," BWV 654; "Komm, Gott Schöpfer, Heiliger Geist," BWV 667
Harry Hodge (strings)	*J. S. Bach: Organ Choral Preludes Arranged for Strings by Harry Hodge.* 2 vols. Glasgow, 1926.	"Schmücke dich, o liebe Seele," BWV 654; "Nun komm, der Heiden Heiland," BWV 659
Mabel Wood-Hill (orchestra)	*An Wasserflüssen Babylon: Chorale Prelude by J. S. Bach.* London, 1926.	"An Wasserflüssen Babylon," BWV 653
William Murdoch (piano)	*J. S. Bach: Organ Choral Preludes Arranged for Pianoforte by William Murdoch.* 4 vols. London, 1928.	"Herr Jesu Christ, dich zu uns wend," BWV 655; "Jesus Christus, unser Heiland," BWV 666

Transcriber and Instrumentation	Bibliographical Citation	Title and BWV No. of Chorale(s) Transcribed
W. Gillies Whittaker (piano)	*J. S. Bach: Thirty-five Chorale Preludes Arranged and Edited for Pianoforte by W. Gillies Whittaker.* 4 vols. London, 1931.	"O Lamm Gottes, unschuldig," BWV 656 (first two verses); "Jesus Christus, unser Heiland," BWV 666
Wilhelm Kempff (piano)	*Musik des Barock und Rokoko, für Klavier übertragen von Wilhelm Kempff.* Berlin, 1932.	"Nun komm, der Heiden Heiland," BWV 659
Leopold Stokowski (orchestra)	(unpublished; recorded on April 7, 1934)	"Nun komm, der Heiden Heiland," BWV 659
Mabel Wood-Hill (string quartet or string orchestra)	*J. S. Bach: Chorale Preludes.* Boston, 1935.	"An Wasserflüssen Babylon," BWV 653
Felix Guenther (piano)	*Johann Sebastian Bach: Twenty-four Choral Preludes Compiled and Arranged for Piano Solo by Felix Guenther.* New York, 1942.	"Komm, Heiliger Geist, Herre Gott," BWV 651; "An Wasserflüssen Babylon," BWV 653b; "Nun danket alle Gott," BWV 657; "Vor deinen Thron tret ich hiermit," BWV 668
Felix Oberborbeck (piano, choir, and various instrumental ensembles)	*Choral: Vor deinen Thron tret ich hiermit (Wenn wir in höchsten Nöten sein), für den praktischen Gebrauch eingerichtet von Felix Oberborbeck.* Wolfenbüttel, 1950.	"Vor deinen Thron tret ich hiermit" BWV 668
Ralph Vaughan Williams (cello and strings)	(unpublished; performed in London on December 28, 1956)	"Schmücke dich, o liebe Seele," BWV 654
Philip Hii (guitar)	*Nun Komm' der Heiden Heiland, BWV 659.* San Francisco, 1996.	"Nun komm, der Heiden Heiland," BWV 659

normally assigned all three upper parts. And since the distance between the soprano and tenor rarely exceeds a tenth, the right hand usually plays these three voices without any alteration. The challenge, as duly observed by Busoni in a footnote, is to accentuate the soprano chorale melody while keeping everything else "well in the background."[40]

Example 5-6 illustrates the first phrase only. Other than the octave doublings in the left hand, the only noteworthy change to the music per se is the addition of a left-hand bass voice that starts on the last beat of measure 4 (on d) and ends a beat and a half later. But Busoni leaves his own indelible print through copious performance instructions (affecting

EXAMPLE 5-6. "Nun komm, der Heiden Heiland," BWV 659, as transcribed for piano by Ferruccio Busoni. © 1898, 1925 Breitkopf & Härtel, Wiesbaden—Leipzig. Used by permission.

tempo, dynamics, articulation, fingering, and pedaling) not found in Bach's score. The result is great expressivity—and gorgeous piano writing.

These two qualities also characterize Max Reger's transcriptions, published two years later. Whereas Busoni admired Bach's organ chorales for their wealth of "art, feeling, and fantasy," his friend Reger detected in them parallels to Richard Wagner, the benchmark for all composers of the era. To quote from the preface of Reger's collection, "Here Bach betrays a depth, a genius in his conception and interpretation of the text which forcibly resembles R. Wagner's grand style." For Reger, then, who likened Bach's organ chorales to "symphonic poems in miniature," the programmatic element in the music was paramount.

Interestingly, Reger undertook these transcriptions at a time (the first half of 1898) of creative paralysis in his budding compositional career, having failed financially and suffering from alcoholism and depression.[41] But something in these organ chorales had a rejuvenative effect on the twenty-five-year-old, since upon their completion he began to compose at a feverish pace, producing over the next two years almost a dozen major organ works, including the Fantasy and Fugue on B-A-C-H. These compositions had far-reaching significance for Reger, for they allowed him to develop his own musical language (an inimitable blend of post-Wagnerian chromaticism and Bachian counterpoint) and to establish his reputation as an important composer. His dramatic recovery, of course, brings to mind Mendelssohn's famous remark about "Schmücke dich," a work, incidentally, transcribed by Reger. Fittingly, Reger's lifelong credo was "B-A-C-H is the beginning and end of all music."

THE TWENTIETH CENTURY

In considering the reception of the Great Eighteen in the present century, let us begin with France. From the mid-1800s on, French organists had regularly played Bach's free organ works, but it was not until the turn of the twentieth century that they performed his chorale settings with any frequency. Various factors account for this neglect, beginning with anti-Protestant sentiment in general and the difficulty of incorporating Lutheran hymns into the Catholic liturgy. Perhaps a more daunting obstacle, however, was simply that most of these musicians did not understand the German language well enough to fully appreciate the chorale texts being set or the manner in which Bach's music enhances these texts.

In this regard, César Franck and Alexandre Guilmant qualify as trail-blazers. Upon his appointment in 1872 as organ professor at the Paris Conservatory, Franck broadened the examination and competition repertory to include not only fugues by Bach but preludes, toccatas, and chorale arrangements as well.[42] More pertinent to this discussion, Franck's pupils were required to play the Great Eighteen setting of "O Lamm Gottes."

Franck also edited this piece, along with the Great Eighteen setting of "An Wasserflüssen Babylon," for a Braille publication of Bach organ works issued in 1887 for the National Institute for Blind Youths.[43] This anthology includes Franck's fingerings and pedalings for both compositions, as well as his registration for "An Wasserflüssen." In accordance with French practice, the former achieve a decidedly legato touch. As for "An Wasserflüssen," Franck recommended a reed stop for the solo line and a "flûte" for the accompaniment—essentially how the work tends to be played today.

Guilmant's knowledge of Bach's organ chorales was unusually comprehensive for a French organist of the period. As organist at the Church of La Trinité in Paris from 1871 to 1901, Guilmant regularly based his plainsong improvisations on chorale settings by Bach, just as he took these works as models for his published compositions. One of these borrows note-for-note from the first Great Eighteen setting of "Allein Gott."[44]

After his death in 1890, Franck was succeeded at the conservatory by Charles Marie Widor, probably the staunchest Bachian France has ever produced. The influence of Bach's organ music is apparent throughout Widor's ten organ symphonies, and certain movements may reflect the Great Eighteen chorales in particular.[45] Yet even Widor confessed in 1899 to his pupil Albert Schweitzer that the more he studied Bach's organ chorales, the less he understood them.[46] Schweitzer's solution was simply to explain to his teacher the meaning of the chorale texts, which proved to be for Widor an epiphany. Because of Widor's preeminence, this episode serves as a turning point in the reception history of Bach's organ chorales in France.

To judge from Schweitzer's monograph on Bach, first published in 1905, it was not the Great Eighteen or Part III of the *Clavierübung* but rather the *Orgelbüchlein* that represented to him the very epitome of that composer's chorale settings for organ. And we read in chapter 3 about Schweitzer's disdain for "long" chorale arrangements. Still, as Stefan Hanheide has revealed, as a recitalist Schweitzer actually preferred the Great Eighteen chorales, particularly "An Wasserflüssen Babylon," "Schmücke dich," "O Lamm Gottes," the first setting of "Nun komm," and "Vor deinen Thron."[47] Clearly, what Schweitzer found appealing about these works was their meditative, mystical ambience and, in the case of "O Lamm Gottes," their remarkably precise text painting.

Another Widor pupil was Marcel Dupré, who effectively inaugurated his career as a concert organist in 1920 by playing the complete organ works of Bach (from memory, of course) in a series of ten recitals at the conservatory.[48] Like Schweitzer, Dupré would go on to publish his own edition of the complete Bach works. Whether Dupré also had favorite pieces from the Great Eighteen is unclear, but "Vor deinen Thron" was played at his funeral.

As evidence that the Great Eighteen enjoyed popularity outside organ circles in the early 1900s, we may look to Arnold Schoenberg. A serious student of Bach's music his entire life, Schoenberg published his orchestral transcriptions of the Great Eighteen settings of "Schmücke dich" and "Komm, Gott Schöpfer" in 1925. He actually prepared these arrangements, however, in the spring of 1922, at the very time he was developing the twelve-tone technique that would so dramatically alter composition in the twentieth century. As the Schoenberg expert Walter Frisch has written:

> The simultaneity of these very different activities may seem odd. But throughout his career Schoenberg was concerned—indeed, obsessed—with the German musical tradition, in which he saw himself having a place. Willi Reich, one of his biographers, was right to dub him a "conservative revolutionary."[49]

Schoenberg's initial encounter with this music goes back at least to June 1918, at which time he was planning on orchestrations not only of these two works but also of three other Great Eighteen chorales ("An Wasserflüssen Babylon," "O Lamm Gottes," and the second setting of "Allein Gott") and the Schübler chorale "Meine Seele erhebt den Herren."[50] To judge from the many inscriptions found in his copy of the Peters edition, Schoenberg's study of these pieces was hardly casual. In the score of "Schmücke dich," for instance, he inserted the first stanza of the chorale text above the right-hand voice and realized various ornamental symbols in the part. He also questioned (for whatever reasons) whether the pedal eighth notes in measure 77 should not read d–f–e-flat–g, even though his published transcription follows Bach's reading here.

The goal of these two arrangements was to elucidate Bach's complex counterpoint. As Schoenberg put it himself, his aim was "to make the individual lines clearer" by the "clarification of the *motivic* procedures in both horizontal and vertical dimensions."[51] Toward this end, the various motives present in Bach's accompanimental voices are played by different instruments, ranging from double bass to piccolo (presumably what Schoenberg meant by "vertical dimensions"). These motives are also distinguished from one another through detailed phrasing, articulation, and dynamics ("horizontal dimensions"). Such specificity, which is clearly along the lines of the *Klangfarbenmelodie* of Schoenberg's Five Orchestral Pieces, op. 16, is of course impossible on a single instrument played by a single performer. But it is especially so on the organ, because of the instrument's limitations with respect to dynamics.

To cite just one example, consider Schoenberg's treatment of the main ritornello theme of "Schmücke dich," as played by the right hand in measures 1–4 (see Example 5-7).[52] Here each of the three motives contained in this melody is assigned to a different group of instruments. The first one, which ends on the downbeat of measure 2, is played by English horns and E-flat clarinets; the second, which comprises all the notes of measure 2, is played by flutes, B-flat clarinets, and celesta; and the third, which begins on the last note of measure 2 and extends to the downbeat of measure 4, is played by oboes. Schoenberg's "analysis," therefore, reveals not only three different motives per se but also dovetailing between the first and second and between the second and third. Only with multiple instruments are these overlaps actually audible.

Both orchestrations also contain much music not found in the organ versions, including entire lines and counterpoints of Schoenberg's own composition. But even this material is intended to "clarify" Bach's

EXAMPLE 5-7. "Schmücke dich, o liebe Seele," BWV 654

polyphony. In "Schmücke dich," for example, Schoenberg obviously interprets the last pedal note of measure 3 and the first of measure 4 as forming their own descending-fifth motive: these two notes are the only played by the double bass in the first four bars and are slurred together in the score. He next adds in measures 7–8 two statements of this figure (played both times by piccolo, flute, B-flat clarinet, and viola) not found in the organ version by inverting the two ascending-fourth motives in the left hand. Here, then, "clarification" is achieved though the motivic implications of the model.

As if to complement the "pointillistic" style of the accompaniment, the ornamented chorale melody is performed throughout by a single instrument, a solo cello, which plays this part exactly as notated by Bach. It may or may not be coincidental that over thirty years later Ralph Vaughan Williams transcribed the same chorale for solo cello and strings in honor of the eightieth birthday of the cellist Pablo Casals.[53] By choosing Bach, Vaughan Williams was paying homage to Casals's favorite composer and perhaps his own as well.[54] Regrettably, this transcription has been neither published nor recorded.

A rather famous but still unpublished orchestration of a Great Eighteen chorale is that by Leopold Stokowski of the first setting of "Nun komm." The great conductor was himself a professional organist, and during his long tenure with the Philadelphia Orchestra he transcribed for that ensemble many of Bach's organ compositions, including chorale settings as well as free works. Whereas Stokowski compared the latter to "daring flights of imagination," he valued Bach's organ chorales—and this one in particular—for their "mystical beauty" and "concentrated essence of deep musical emotion."[55]

In stark contrast to Schoenberg's motivic-fragmentation technique, Stokowski was content to preserve all four voices of his model more or less exactly as Bach wrote them. Nor did Stokowski add any material whatsoever of his own invention. Thus, while Schoenberg's arrangements qualify as true recompositions, Stokowski's is a transcription in the strictest sense of the word.

Surely one reason he chose this chorale was its unusual walking-bass pedal line, which seems idiomatically conceived for strings rather than organ. Accordingly, this part is played throughout by double bass and second cello, pizzicato. Muted violas and first cellos take the alto and tenor voices, respectively. And the embellished chorale melody found in the soprano is sounded in succession by various woodwind instruments (phrases 1–3) and muted violins (phrase 4). No doubt the subdued nature of this scoring heightens the work's "mystical beauty," just as this Advent chorale evokes the mystery of the Incarnation.[56]

Stokowski's score, not surprisingly, contains all manner of instructions vis-à-vis articulation and dynamics that create a quintessentially Romantic expressivity.[57] His ultra-rubato approach to tempo also contributes to this effect, as do the constant string glissandos heard in his 1934 recording.[58] The purist may frown, but the sheer musicality of the performance, not to mention the beauty of the orchestral sound, is beyond dispute.

As for other twentieth-century transcriptions of this chorale, that by Wilhelm Kempff adopts a piano texture very similar to Busoni's. In performing his transcription, though, Kempff greatly accentuated the tenor line of measure 21 in what appears to be an allusion to "O Sacred Head, Now Wounded."[59] The idea behind Philip Hii's recent guitar transcription, conversely, seems to be to transfer as much material as the limited polyphonic capabilities of this instrument allow—quite a challenge considering the wide range and four-voice texture of the model. This normally means conflating two voices to form one. But so skillful is the adaptation that the listener rarely senses that anything is missing.[60]

The twentieth century has witnessed far more transcriptions of the Great Eighteen chorales than any previous era. As the music has grown in popularity over the last 100 years, so has the demand for it in a wide variety of instrumentations. These works owe their unprecedented renown today of course to the transcendent, enduring power of the music itself. But certain external agents have aided in this process as well, especially the increasing availability of performing editions of and scholarly writings on the collection and advances in recording technology that have allowed for the music's mass dissemination. Who knows what the new millennium will bring?

NOTES

CHAPTER 1

1. Peter Williams, *The Organ Music of J. S. Bach*, 3 vols. (Cambridge: Cambridge University Press, 1980–84), 2:127.

2. See Robert L. Marshall, "Chorale Settings," in *The New Grove Dictionary of Music and Musicians*, edited by Stanley Sadie (London: Macmillan, 1980), 4:329–30.

3. On these manuscripts, see Hermann Zietz, *Quellenkritische Untersuchungen an den Bach-Handschriften P 801, P 802 und P 803 aus dem "Krebs'schen Nachlass" unter besonderer Berücksichtigung der Choralbearbeitungen des jungen J. S. Bach* (Hamburg: Karl Dieter Wagner, 1969); Stephen Daw, "Copies of J. S. Bach by Walther and Krebs: A Study of the Manuscripts P 801, P 802, and P 803," *Organ Yearbook* 7 (1976): 31–58; and Kirsten Beisswenger, "Zur Chronologie der Notenhandschriften Johann Gottfried Walthers," in *Acht kleine Präludien und Studien über BACH: Georg von Dadelsen zum 70. Geburtstag am 17. November 1988,* edited by the Johann-Sebastian-Bach-Institut, Göttingen (Wiesbaden: Breitkopf & Härtel, 1992), 11–39.

4. Jean-Claude Zehnder, "Georg Böhm und Johann Sebastian Bach: Zur Chronologie der Bachschen Stilentwicklung," *Bach-Jahrbuch* 74 (1988): 73–110, and "Zu Bachs Stilentwicklung in der Mühlhäuser und Weimarer Zeit," in *Das Frühwerk Johann Sebastian Bachs*, edited by Karl Heller and Hans-Joachim Schulze (Cologne: Studio, 1995), 311–38.

5. In addition to the articles listed in n. 4, see Jean-Claude Zehnder, "Die Weimarer Orgelmusik Johann Sebastian Bachs im Spiegel seiner Kantaten," *Musik und Gottesdienst* 41 (1987): 149–62, "Giuseppe Torelli und Johann Sebastian Bach: Zu Bachs Weimarer Konzertform," *Bach-Jahrbuch* 77 (1991): 33–95, and "Zum späten Weimarer Stil Johann Sebastian Bachs," in *Bachs*

Orchesterwerke: Bericht über das 1. Dortmunder Bach-Symposion 1996, edited by Martin Geck (Witten: Klangfarben-Musikverlag, 1997), 89–124.

6. See Christoph Wolff et al., *The New Grove Bach Family* (New York: Norton, 1983), 124.

7. Because of its "migratory" bass line, this work is printed in the *Neue Bach-Ausgabe* on only two staves, with pedal cues; see NBA IV/2 (*Die Orgelchoräle aus der Leipziger Originalhandschrift*), edited by Hans Klotz. See also NBA IV/2, KB, 83; and Williams, *The Organ Music*, 2:165.

8. See Zehnder, "Georg Böhm," 100–101; and Henning Müller-Buscher, *Georg Böhms Choralbearbeitungen für Tasteninstrumente* (Laaber: Laaber-Verlag, 1979), 95–105. Henceforth, any mention of Bach's relationship to Böhm is based on Zehnder's article.

9. See Johann Michael Bach, *Sämtliche Orgelchoräle / The Complete Organ Chorales*, edited by Christoph Wolff (Neuhausen-Stuttgart: Hänssler, 1988); and Dietrich Buxtehude, *Sämtliche Orgelwerke*, edited by Josef Hedar, 4 vols. (Copenhagen: Wilhelm Hansen, 1952), 4:14–19. Buxtehude supplies an interlude only between Variations 1 and 2.

10. See Christoph Wolff, ed., *The Neumeister Collection of Chorale Preludes from the Bach Circle*, facsimile edition (New Haven: Yale University Press, 1986), 8–9.

11. See Russell Stinson, "The Compositional History of Bach's *Orgelbüchlein* Reconsidered," *Bach Perspectives* 1 (1995): 43–78.

12. See Laurence Dreyfus, *Bach and the Patterns of Invention* (Cambridge, Mass.: Harvard University Press, 1996), 118.

13. See Hans T. David and Arthur Mendel, *The New Bach Reader: A Life of Johann Sebastian Bach in Letters and Documents*, revised and enlarged by Christoph Wolff (New York: Norton, 1998), 300.

14. See Stinson, "The Compositional History."

15. See Lawrence Archbold, "Towards a Critical Understanding of Buxtehude's Expressive Chorale Preludes," in *Church, Stage, and Studio: Music and Its Contexts in Seventeenth-Century Germany*, edited by Paul Walker (Ann Arbor: UMI Research Press, 1990), 103–4.

16. See Russell Stinson, *Bach: The Orgelbüchlein* (New York: Schirmer, 1996; reprint, New York: Oxford University Press, 1999) 19–21.

17. Throughout this book, we will follow the measure numbering of the *Neue Bach-Ausgabe*, the standard edition of Bach's music, despite its quirky practice of two different sets of measure numbers for repeated passages.

18. See Yoshitake Kobayashi, "Quellenkundliche Überlegungen zur Chronologie der Weimarer Vokalwerke Bachs," in Heller and Schulze, *Das Frühwerk Johann Sebastian Bachs*, 296–97.

19. As we will discuss in the next chapter, the version of this work with the chorale melody in the soprano, cataloged as BWV 653b (double-pedal arrangement), is of doubtful authenticity.

20. See NBA IV/1 (*Orgelbüchlein; Sechs Choräle von verschiedener Art [Schübler-Choräle]; Orgelpartiten*), edited by Heinz-Harald Löhlein, KB, 87;

and Yoshitake Kobayashi, *Die Notenschrift Johann Sebastian Bachs: Dokumentation ihrer Entwicklung* (NBA IX/2), 38.

21. See Willi Apel, *The History of Keyboard Music to 1700,* translated and revised by Hans Tischler (Bloomington: Indiana University Press, 1972), 656–57.

22. See Hans-Joachim Schulze, "J. S. Bach's Concerto-Arrangements for Organ–Studies or Commissioned Works?" *Organ Yearbook* 3 (1972): 4–13, and *Studien zur Bach-Überlieferung im 18. Jahrhundert* (Leipzig: Edition Peters, 1984), 155–63.

23. See George B. Stauffer, *The Organ Preludes of Johann Sebastian Bach* (Ann Arbor: UMI Research Press, 1980), 46–58.

24. See Werner Breig, "The 'Great Eighteen' Chorales: Bach's Revisional Process and the Genesis of the Work," in *J. S. Bach as Organist: His Instruments, Music, and Performance Practices*, edited by George Stauffer and Ernest May (Bloomington: Indiana University Press, 1986), 104–10.

25. Werner Breig, "Bachs Orgelchoral und die italienische Instrumentalmusik," in *Bach und die italienische Musik*, edited by Wolfgang Osthoff and Reinhard Wiesend (Venice: Centro Tedesco di Studi Veneziani, 1987), 99.

26. This is especially true with regard to the abbreviated (and obviously corrupt) versions of these two pieces found in the manuscript SBB Mus. ms. 30377. Penned by an anonymous scribe during the second half of the eighteenth century, this source completely omits from each work the concluding cantus firmus–chorale section. The copyist may not have even realized he was notating chorale settings, since in neither instance did he inscribe a chorale title, merely the generic heading "Trio." This version of "Herr Jesu Christ" is cataloged as BWV 655c. On the scribe and date of this manuscript, see NBA V/6.2 (*Das Wohltemperierte Klavier II; Fünf Praeludien und Fughetten*), edited by Alfred Dürr, KB, 121.

27. See Williams, *The Organ Music*, 2:154.

28. See Kobayashi, *Die Notenschrift Johann Sebastian Bachs*, 207.

29. See Wolff et al., *The New Grove Bach Family*, 122.

CHAPTER 2

1. See Alfred Dürr, "Heinrich Nicolaus Gerber als Schüler Bachs," *Bach-Jahrbuch* 64 (1978): 7–18.

2. For a physical description, see NBA IV/7 (*Sechs Sonaten und verschiedene Einzelwerke*), edited by Dietrich Kilian, KB, 17–22.

3. On the dating of these sources, see Yoshitake Kobayashi, *Die Notenschrift Johann Sebastian Bachs: Dokumentation ihrer Entwicklung* (NBA IX/2), 206–7, and "Zur Chronologie der Spätwerke Johann Sebastian Bachs: Kompositions- und Aufführungstätigkeit von 1736 bis 1750," *Bach-Jahrbuch* 74 (1988): 45, 56–57.

4. Georg von Dadelsen, *Beiträge zur Chronologie der Werke Johann Sebastian Bachs* (Trossingen: Hohner, 1958), 109–10.

5. Kobayashi, "Zur Chronologie der Spätwerke," 45, 56–57, and *Die Notenschrift Johann Sebastian Bachs*, 207.

6. See Kobayashi, "Zur Chronologie der Spätwerke," 60.

7. See Yoshitake Kobayashi, "Zur Teilung des Bachschen Erbes," in *Acht kleine Präludien und Studien über BACH: Georg von Dadelsen zum 70. Geburtstag am 17. November 1988*, edited by the Johann-Sebastian-Bach-Institut, Göttingen (Wiesbaden: Breitkopf & Härtel, 1992), 69.

8. See Peter Wollny, "Zur Überlieferung der Instrumentalwerke Johann Sebastian Bachs: Der Quellenbesitz Carl Philipp Emanuel Bachs," *Bach-Jahrbuch* 82 (1996): 12–13.

9. See the preface to Johann Sebastian Bach, *Die achtzehn grossen Orgelchoräle BWV 651–668 und Canonische Veränderungen über "Vom Himmel hoch" BWV 769*, facsimile edition of the autograph manuscript, with a preface by Peter Wollny (Laaber: Laaber-Verlag, 1999).

10. The barely visible inscription *Von Altnikols Hand* at the top of Figure 2–2 was penned by Georg Poelchau, the owner of this manuscript in the early nineteenth century; see Clark Kelly, "Johann Sebastian Bach's 'Eighteen' Chorales, BWV 651–668: Perspectives on Editions and Hymnology" (D.M.A. dissertation, Eastman School of Music, 1988), 87.

11. Georg von Dadelsen, *Bemerkungen zur Handschrift Johann Sebastian Bachs, seiner Familie und seines Kreises* (Trossingen: Hohner, 1957), 16.

12. See Russell Stinson, "The Compositional History of Bach's Orgelbüchlein Reconsidered," *Bach Perspectives* 1 (1995): 67–69.

13. Christoph Wolff, "The Deathbed Chorale: Exposing a Myth," in Wolff, *Bach: Essays on His Life and Music* (Cambridge, Mass.: Harvard University Press, 1991), 272–94.

14. See Detlev Kranemann, "Johann Sebastian Bachs Krankheit und Todesursache—Versuch einer Deutung," *Bach-Jahrbuch* 76 (1990): 59–60.

15. Regarding the inscriptions beneath the last system, the series of numbers to the left, whose meaning is uncertain, is in an unknown hand, obviously not that of the copyist. To the right is an addition by Siegfried Wilhelm Dehn, who was the music librarian of the Königliche Bibliothek in Berlin shortly after the library came into possession of this manuscript in 1841: *Fragment des Chorals, der in der "Kunst der Fuge" mit dem Text "Wenn wir in höchsten Nöten" vorkommt* (Fragment of the chorale that occurs in the "Art of Fugue" with the text "Wenn wir in höchsten Nöten"). See Alfred Dürr, *Johann Sebastian Bach: Seine Handschrift—Abbild seines Schaffens* (Wiesbaden: Breitkopf & Härtel, 1984), commentary to Blatt 79.

16. Robert L. Marshall, *The Compositional Process of J. S. Bach: A Study of the Autograph Scores of the Vocal Works*, 2 vols. (Princeton: Princeton University Press, 1972), 1:4–5.

17. See NBA IV/2, KB, 14. In addition to being rather superficial, Klotz's commentary is riddled with major factual mistakes, such as the statement (on p. 59) that the manuscript SBB P 801 contains an autograph "sketch" of "Komm, Gott Schöpfer." Moreover, Klotz's edition abounds in questionable

readings; on this point, see Kelly, "Johann Sebastian Bach's 'Eighteen' Chorales," 31–104.

18. Bach's general—and parsimonious—practice in scoring organ music was to employ a separate pedal staff only for trio compositions (see Figure 2–1). In the autograph of the Great Eighteen, he was also forced to adopt this procedure for certain works whose left-hand staff he notated in alto or tenor clef (see Figure 2–7). He did the same for "Von Gott will ich nicht lassen," whose left-hand staff is in bass clef, obviously because this work's pedal line—a tenor part—would have been greatly obscured by the busy and wide-ranging bass and alto voices. But one is puzzled by Bach's use of a separate pedal staff for the third setting of "Nun komm," whose left-hand staff is likewise in bass clef. In that work, much like the first setting of "Komm, Heiliger Geist," the pedal part never crosses any voice played by the left hand, and its slow rhythms make it visually distinct as well. Adding it to the bottom of the left-hand staff would have created no confusion whatever.

19. See Johann Sebastian Bach, *Fantasia super Komm Heiliger Geist*, facsimile edition of the autograph, with a preface by Peter Wackernagel (Leipzig: Edition Merseburger, 1950).

20. See Johann Sebastian Bach, *Orgelbüchlein, 18 grosse Choralbearbeitungen, Anhang: Varianten,* edited by Heinz Lohmann (Wiesbaden: Breitkopf & Härtel, 1968). Lohmann furnishes such alternate readings for many of the chorales, which makes his edition a handy tool for studying Bach's revisions in these pieces. Still, his edition by no means prints all the discrepant readings, and it provides the complete scores only of those early versions (six to be exact) that differ most substantially from the revised ones. The *Neue Bach-Ausgabe* remains the only complete edition of the early versions.

21. See NBA IV/2, KB, 40; and verse 3 of Walther's setting of "Schmücke dich, o liebe Seele," in Johann Gottfried Walther, *Ausgewählte Orgelwerke*, edited by Heinz Lohmann, 3 vols. (Wiesbaden: Breitkopf & Härtel, 1966), 2:163–65.

22. The revision in measure 11, beat 2, where the two versions fully agree, is obviously not compositional but the result of a copying error.

23. See, for example, Werner Breig, "The 'Great Eighteen' Chorales: Bach's Revisional Process and the Genesis of the Work," in *J. S. Bach as Organist: His Instruments, Music, and Performance Practices*, edited by George Stauffer and Ernest May (Bloomington: Indiana University Press, 1986), 110–18.

24. See Robert L. Marshall, liner notes to *The Uncommon Bach: Johann Sebastian Bach Organ Works—Variants, Rarities, and Transcriptions* (Pro Gloria Musicae Recordings, PGM 115, 1997).

25. Performers of this version, incidentally, should beware of older editions, such as the Peters, that print the text of Walther's copy as altered by an unknown nineteenth-century hand; see NBA IV/2, KB, 68. Two editions that offer the unaltered text are Lohmann's and the *Neue Bach-Ausgabe*.

26. For a comparison, see Example 5–5.

27. Bach also used the "incorrect" notation of half notes divided into eighth-note triplets in the famous *Orgelbüchlein* setting of "In dulci jubilo."

28. Two early versions of this work complex exist: one known as BWV 664a, which appears in the Peters and Bachgesellschaft editions; and another known as BWV 664b, which was published for the first time in the *Neue Bach-Ausgabe*. The differences between the two are trifling, and many of them may be due merely to scribal mistakes. But it does seem clear enough that BWV 664b represents the original version, from which BWV 664a was adapted. See NBA IV/2, KB, 82–83; and Peter Williams, *The Organ Music of J. S. Bach*, 3 vols. (Cambridge: Cambridge University Press, 1980–84), 2:163–64.

29. See Christoph Wolff et al., *The New Grove Bach Family* (New York: Norton, 1983), 167.

CHAPTER 3

1. Manfred F. Bukofzer, *Music in the Baroque Era: From Monteverdi to Bach* (New York: Norton, 1947), 299.

2. Albert Schweitzer, *J. S. Bach*, translated by Ernest Newman, 2 vols. (New York: Macmillan, 1925; reprint, New York: Dover, 1966), 1:291, 2:61–62.

3. Harvey Grace, *The Organ Works of Bach* (London: Novello, 1922), 263.

4. Philipp Spitta, *Johann Sebastian Bach: His Work and Influence on the Music of Germany, 1685–1750*, translated by Clara Bell and J. A. Fuller-Maitland, 3 vols. (London: Novello, 1889; reprint, New York: Dover, 1952), 1:611.

5. See Malcolm Boyd, *Bach*, rev. ed. (New York: Schirmer, 1997), 36.

6. See Hans T. David and Arthur Mendel, *The New Bach Reader: A Life of Johann Sebastian Bach in Letters and Documents*, revised and enlarged by Christoph Wolff (New York: Norton, 1998), 300.

7. See Robin A. Leaver, "Bach and Hymnody: The Evidence of the *Orgelbüchlein*," *Early Music* 13 (1985): 227–36.

8. See Peter Williams, *The Organ Music of J. S. Bach*, 3 vols. (Cambridge: Cambridge University Press, 1980–84), 2:78, 157–58; and Clark Kelly, "Johann Sebastian Bach's 'Eighteen' Chorales, BWV 651–668: Perspectives on Editions and Hymnology" (D.M.A. dissertation, Eastman School of Music, 1988), 176.

9. See Robin A. Leaver, liner notes to *The Leipzig Chorales of J. S. Bach: Joan Lippincott, Organist* (Gothic Records, G 49099, 1998). Leaver's statement that Bach inscribed the letters "SDG" (for his motto, "Soli Deo Gloria") at the end of his autograph entry of the third "Allein Gott" setting is clearly wrong. The same mistake appears in Williams, *The Organ Music*, 2:162.

10. Figure 3–1 is based on Williams, *The Organ Music*, 3:124–25; and Winfried Schrammek, "Orgel, Positiv, Clavicymbel und Glocken der Schlosskirche zu Weimar 1658 bis 1774," in *Bericht über die Wissenschaftliche Konferenz zum V. Internationalen Bachfest der DDR in Verbindung mit dem 60. Bachfest der Neuen Bachgesellschaft*, edited by Winfried Hoffmann and Armin Schneiderheinze (Leipzig: VEB Deutscher Verlag für Musik, 1988), 99–111. According to Schrammek's investigation of Weimar court records, when the

organ was first rebuilt (in 1707–8) it acquired the manual and pedal compasses given in Figure 3–1. These compasses remained unchanged until 1774, when the organ, along with the entire court chapel, was destroyed by fire.

11. See Williams, *The Organ Music*, 3:118–19; and Lynn Edwards, "The Thuringian Organ 1702–1720: ' . . . ein wohlgerathenes gravitätisches Werk,'" *Organ Yearbook* 22 (1991): 119–50.

12. Barbara Owen, *The Registration of Baroque Organ Music* (Bloomington: Indiana University Press, 1997), 162.

13. See Williams, *The Organ Music*, 3:140–41.

14. Date according to Schrammek, "Orgel, Positiv," 99. For a detailed discussion of the chapel's construction, see Reinhold Jauernig, "Johann Sebastian Bach in Weimar: Neue Forschungsergebnisse aus Weimarer Quellen," in *Johann Sebastian Bach in Thüringen: Festgabe zum Gedenkjahr 1950*, edited by Heinrich Besseler and Günther Kraft (Weimar: Thüringer Volksverlag, 1950), 58–71.

15. On the date of this print, see Gregory G. Butler, "Neues zur Datierung der Goldberg-Variationen," *Bach-Jahrbuch* 74 (1988): 219–23.

16. See David and Mendel, *The New Bach Reader*, 281–94.

17. Dates according to Yoshitake Kobayashi, "Zur Chronologie der Spätwerke Johann Sebastian Bachs: Kompositions- und Aufführungstätigkeit von 1736 bis 1750," *Bach-Jahrbuch* 74 (1988): 41–61.

18. See Christoph Wolff et al., *The New Grove Bach Family* (New York: Norton, 1983), 165.

19. See Alfred Dürr, "Bach's Chorale Cantatas," in *Cantors at the Crossroads: Essays on Church Music in Honor of Walter E. Buszin*, edited by Johannes Riedel (St. Louis: Concordia, 1967), 111.

20. See Gregory G. Butler, *Bach's Clavier-Übung III: The Making of a Print. With a Companion Study of the Canonic Variations on "Vom Himmel Hoch," BWV 769* (Durham, N. C.: Duke University Press, 1990), 103.

21. NBA IV/2, KB, 13.

22. See NBA IV/2, KB, 15; and NBA IV/7, KB, 17.

23. See Barbara Owen, *E. Power Biggs: Concert Organist* (Bloomington: Indiana University Press, 1987), 42.

24. See, for instance, the recording by Joan Lippincott cited in n. 9.

25. Butler, *Bach's Clavier-Übung III*, 83–85.

26. Christoph Wolff, "Principles of Design and Order in Bach's Original Editions," in Wolff, *Bach: Essays on His Life and Music* (Cambridge, Mass.: Harvard University Press, 1991), 345.

27. Robert L. Marshall, *Luther, Bach, and the Early Reformation Chorale* (Kessler Reformation Lecture, Emory University, 1995), 2.

28. See NBA IV/2, KB, 59.

29. See Marshall, *Luther, Bach, and the Early Reformation Chorale*, 2.

30. In the case of the *Clavierübung*, the presence of three "Allein Gott" settings must also be understood in connection with the two triple groupings of Kyrie texts that precede it; see Wolff, "Principles of Design and Order," 345–46.

31. See Christoph Wolff, "Bach and the Tradition of the Palestrina Style," in Wolff, *Bach: Essays on His Life and Music*, 92–104.

32. See Williams, *The Organ Music*, 2:135.

CHAPTER 4

1. For complete translations of all the hymns set in the Great Eighteen, see Mark S. Bighley, *The Lutheran Chorales in the Organ Works of J. S. Bach* (St. Louis: Concordia, 1986). Translations of first stanzas are found in Peter Williams, *The Organ Music of J. S. Bach*, 3 vols. (Cambridge: Cambridge University Press, 1980–84); and Hermann Keller, *The Organ Works of Bach: A Contribution to their History, Form, Interpretation and Performance*, translated by Helen Hewitt (New York: C. F. Peters, 1967). In following the piece-by-piece commentaries in the present chapter, the reader may find it helpful to refer to such translations.

2. For example, Wolfgang Rübsam's recent recording lasts a whopping eight minutes and twenty-six seconds; see *J. S. Bach: Organ Chorales from the Leipzig Manuscript*, vol. 1 (Naxos, 8.550901, 1994).

3. See, for instance, the registration instructions given in the once very popular G. Schirmer edition *Twelve Chorale Preludes for Organ by Johann Sebastian Bach*, edited by Franklin Glynn (New York: G. Schirmer, 1931).

4. See George B. Stauffer, *The Organ Preludes of Johann Sebastian Bach* (Ann Arbor: UMI Research Press, 1980), 159–61.

5. See the series of reports in the July 1991 issue of the *Early Keyboard Studies Newsletter*, published by the Westfield Center.

6. See Hans T. David and Arthur Mendel, *The New Bach Reader: A Life of Johann Sebastian Bach in Letters and Documents*, revised and enlarged by Christoph Wolff (New York: Norton, 1998), 336.

7. See David and Mendel, *The New Bach Reader*, 302.

8. See the edition in Johann Adam Reinken, *Sämtliche Orgelwerke*, edited by Klaus Beckmann (Wiesbaden: Breitkopf & Härtel, 1974).

9. See David and Mendel, *The New Bach Reader*, 302.

10. See Christoph Wolff, "Bach and Johann Adam Reinken: A Context for the Early Works," in Wolff, *Bach: Essays on His Life and Music* (Cambridge, Mass.: Harvard University Press, 1991), 56–71.

11. See David and Mendel, *The New Bach Reader*, 364.

12. See Harvey Grace, *The Organ Works of Bach* (London: Novello, 1922), 274.

13. For a performance of this type, see E. Power Biggs's recording of the ornamental chorale "Liebster Jesu, wir sind hier," BWV 731, on *Bach Organ Favorites*, vol. 4 (Columbia Masterworks, MS 7424).

14. As does, for instance, Lionel Rogg in his recording of the Great Eighteen on the Harmonia Mundi label (HMX 290772.83, 1992).

15. See *J. S. Bach Organ Works*, vol. 2: *Leipzig Mastery* (Raven, OAR-300, 1995).

16. The harpsichordist Wanda Landowska reportedly played binary dance movements by Bach in this way; see Imogene Horsley et al., "Improvisation," in *The New Grove Dictionary of Music and Musicians*, edited by Stanley Sadie (London: Macmillan, 1980), 9:42.

17. See *Johann Sebastian Bach Organ Works*, vol. 4 (Musical Heritage Society, MHS Stereo 844775T).

18. See Clark Kelly, "Johann Sebastian Bach's 'Eighteen' Chorales, BWV 651–668: Perspectives on Editions and Hymnology" (D.M.A. dissertation, Eastman School of Music, 1988), 43; and Alfred Dürr, *Johann Sebastian Bach: Seine Handschrift—Abbild seines Schaffens* (Wiesbaden: Breitkopf & Härtel, 1984), commentary to Blatt 9.

19. See Grace, *The Organ Works*, 268; and Keller, *The Organ Works*, 250.

20. Philipp Spitta, *Johann Sebastian Bach: His Work and Influence on the Music of Germany, 1685–1750*, translated by Clara Bell and J. A. Fuller-Maitland, 3 vols. (London: Novello, 1889; reprint, New York: Dover, 1952), 1:612.

21. This passage is especially repetitive in the early version, which contains nothing but sequential quarter notes for the right hand. For other unusually long sequences in Bach's organ music, see measures 9–12 of "Ach Herr, mich armen Sünder," BWV 742; and measures 9–14 of the Adagio movement from the Toccata, Adagio, and Fugue in C Major.

22. For a similar instance of chromatic alteration in one of Bach's chorale partitas, see the first measure of the seventh variation of "Sei gegrüsset, Jesu gütig."

23. Werner Breig, "Der norddeutsche Orgelchoral und Johann Sebastian Bach: Gattung, Typus, Werk," in *Gattung und Werk in der Musikgeschichte Norddeutschlands und Skandinaviens*, edited by Friedhelm Krummacher and Heinrich W. Schwab (Kassel: Bärenreiter, 1982), 92.

24. Spitta, *Johann Sebastian Bach*, 1:612.

25. Thomas Fredric Harmon, *The Registration of J. S. Bach's Organ Works* (Buren: Frits Knuf, 1978), 243.

26. Instead of writing *nicht* here, Bach draws an unusual symbol that was for him a standard abbreviation for this word. For transcriptions, see Kelly, "Johann Sebastian Bach's 'Eighteen' Chorales," 55; and Robert L. Marshall, *The Compositional Process of J. S. Bach: A Study of the Autograph Scores of the Vocal Works*, 2 vols. (Princeton: Princeton University Press, 1972), 2:6.

27. Spitta, *Johann Sebastian Bach*, 1:614.

28. Williams, *The Organ Music*, 2:149.

29. For a facsimile, see NBA IV/2, x.

30. Kelly, "Johann Sebastian Bach's 'Eighteen' Chorales," 56.

31. Grace, *The Organ Works*, 277.

32. See Peter Bondanella, *Italian Cinema: From Neorealism to the Present* (New York: Continuum, 1983), 346.

33. Keller, *The Organ Works*, 254.

34. See Roswitha Bruggaier, "Das Urbild von Johann Sebastian Bachs Choralbearbeitung 'Nun komm, der Heiden Heiland' (BWV 660)—eine

Komposition mit Viola da gamba?" *Bach-Jahrbuch* 73 (1987): 165–68. Ever since this work was published by the Bachgesellschaft, scholars have conjectured that it is some sort of transcription (but, of course, without any documentary evidence).

35. So unusual is this ending that some organists refuse to play it as written, preferring instead to hold the chord and pedal note for the same length; see, for example, Lionel Rogg's recording cited in n. 14. Yet in the autographs of both the early and revised versions, Bach meticulously notates this weird effect.

36. Spitta, *Johann Sebastian Bach*, 1:618.

37. Grace, *The Organ Works*, 271.

38. Keller, *The Organ Works*, 255.

39. Not so, though, in the undoubtedly corrupt version listed as BWV 660b. Whoever prepared this arrangement (J. T. Krebs?) transferred the bottom line to the left hand and the middle line to the right and assigned the feet a greatly simplified rendition (half notes and whole notes) of the top part. This arrangement was obviously fashioned from the early version, BWV 660a. See NBA IV/2, KB, 76–77; and Williams, *The Organ Music*, 2:155.

40. All the other inscriptions on these two pages were made during the nineteenth century by staff members of the Königliche Bibliothek, Berlin; see NBA IV/2, KB, 15.

41. On this point, see Dürr, *Johann Sebastian Bach*, commentary to Blatt 6.

42. Spitta, *Johann Sebastian Bach*, 1:619.

43. Grace, *The Organ Works*, 265.

44. André Pirro, *Johann Sebastian Bach: The Organist and His Works for the Organ*, translated by Wallace Goodrich (New York: G. Schirmer, 1902), 90.

45. See Williams, *The Organ Music*, 2:159.

46. Robert L. Marshall, "Tempo and Dynamics: The Original Terminology," in Marshall, *The Music of Johann Sebastian Bach: The Sources, the Style, the Significance* (New York: Schirmer, 1989), 266, and "Bach's *tempo ordinario*: A Plaine and Easie Introduction to the System," in *Critica Musica: Essays in Honor of Paul Brainard*, edited by John Knowles (New York: Gordon & Beach, 1996), 266.

47. See, for example, Pirro, *Johann Sebastian Bach*, 90–91; and Grace, *The Organ Music*, 274.

48. Spitta, *Johann Sebastian Bach*, 1:615–16; and Keller, *The Organ Works*, 257.

49. See Kelly, "Johann Sebastian Bach's 'Eighteen' Chorales," 75.

50. See Laurence Dreyfus, *Bach and the Patterns of Invention* (Cambridge, Mass.: Harvard University Press, 1996), 123.

51. See Arnold Schoenberg, *Bearbeitungen I/II: Kritischer Bericht, Fragmente*, edited by Rudolf Stephan and Tadeusz Okuljar (Mainz: B. Schott's Söhne; Vienna: Universal Edition AG, 1986–88), xxvi.

52. See Keller, *The Organ Works*, 258.

53. Werner Breig, "Bachs Orgelchoral und die italienische Instrumentalmusik," in *Bach und die italienische Musik*, edited by Wolfgang Osthoff and Reinhard Wiesend (Venice: Centro Tedesco di Studi Veneziani, 1987), 99–104.

54. Spitta, *Johann Sebastian Bach*, 1:613–14. It is hard to accept Albert Schweitzer's theory that the opening two lines of the first stanza are also symbolized in this way; see Schweitzer, *J. S. Bach*, translated by Ernest Newman, 2 vols. (New York: Macmillan, 1925; reprint, New York: Dover, 1966), 2:73–74.

55. Interestingly, the second setting of "Komm, Heiliger Geist" from the Great Eighteen adopts both of these procedures as well. It, too, is a chorale motet.

56. Rather than giving the full title of the chorale, Altnikol writes an abbreviation (*p.*) for the Latin word *perge*, meaning "and so forth." Bach himself also used this abbreviation. See Kelly, "Johann Sebastian Bach's 'Eighteen' Chorales," 87; and Dürr, *Johann Sebastian Bach*, commentary to Blatt 33.

57. Williams, *The Organ Music*, 2:168.

58. See Claudio Spies, "The Organ Supplanted: A Case for Differentiations," *Perspectives of New Music* 11 (Spring–Summer 1973): 32.

59. See Williams, *The Organ Music*, 2:170.

60. Much like Altnikol did for the *manualiter* setting of "Jesus Christus, unser Heiland," this anonymous scribe uses an abbreviation (*pp*) for the Latin word *perge*; see Kelly, "Johann Sebastian Bach's 'Eighteen' Chorales," 97.

61. See Kelly, "Johann Sebastian Bach's 'Eighteen' Chorales," 215; and Bighley, *The Lutheran Chorales*, 232. As Bighley points out, the hymn's placement in the "Death and Eternity" section of the *Evangelisches Kirchengesangbuch* (the modern German Protestant hymnal) is due less to the text itself than its association with Bach's death.

CHAPTER 5

1. For a list of these sources, see NBA IV/2, KB, 16–51.

2. See Russell Stinson, *Bach: The Orgelbüchlein* (New York: Schirmer, 1996; reprint, New York: Oxford University Press, 1999), 145–66.

3. See George B. Stauffer, "J. S. Bach as Organ Pedagogue," in *The Organist as Scholar: Essays in Memory of Russell Saunders*, edited by Kerala J. Snyder (Stuyvesant: Pendragon Press, 1994), 33.

4. See Alfred Dürr, "Heinrich Nicolaus Gerber als Schüler Bachs," *Bach-Jahrbuch* 64 (1978): 7–18, and "Zur Chronologie der Handschrift Johann Christoph Altnickols und Johann Friedrich Agricolas," *Bach-Jahrbuch* 56 (1970): 44–63.

5. See Hans-Joachim Schulze, *Studien zur Bach-Überlieferung im 18. Jahrhundert* (Leipzig: Edition Peters, 1984), 61–68.

6. See Johann Ludwig Krebs, *Choralbearbeitungen*, edited by Gerhard Weinberger (Wiesbaden: Breitkopf & Härtel, 1986).

7. On the Mempell-Preller Collection, see Peter Krause, *Handschriften der Werke Johann Sebastian Bachs in der Musikbibliothek der Stadt Leipzig* (Leipzig: Musikbibliothek der Stadt Leipzig, 1964), 29–42; and Schulze, *Studien zur Bach-Überlieferung*, 69–88.

8. See Ernest May, "Connections between Breitkopf and J. S. Bach," *Bach Perspectives* 2 (*J. S. Bach, the Breitkopfs, and Eighteenth-Century Music Trade*)

(1996): 11–26, and "Breitkopf's Role in the Transmission of J. S. Bach's Organ Chorales" (Ph.D. dissertation, Princeton University, 1974), 79–93; and Clark Kelly, "Johann Sebastian Bach's 'Eighteen' Chorales, BWV 651–668: Perspectives on Editions and Hymnology" (D.M.A. dissertation, Eastman School of Music, 1988), 19–22. How Penzel gained access to these Breitkopf house manuscripts is unclear.

9. See NBA IV/5–6 (*Präludien, Toccaten, Fantasien und Fugen für Orgel*), edited by Dietrich Kilian, KB, 217–20.

10. The other four are listed in Reinmar Emans and Michael Meyer-Frerichs, *Johann Sebastian Bach. Orgelchoräle zweifelhafte Echtheit: Thematischer Katalog* (Göttingen: Johann-Sebastian-Bach-Institut, 1997), 45–47.

11. For a detailed discussion, see Reinmar Emans, "Choralvorspiele J. S. Bachs? Probleme der Zuschreibung und Echtheitskritik, dargestellt an einigen Beispielen aus der Sammlung C 55, Oxford, Bodleian Library" (unpublished paper); and Kirsten Beisswenger, "An Early Version of the First Movement of the *Italian Concerto* BWV 971 from the Scholz Collection?" in *Bach Studies 2*, edited by Daniel R. Melamed (Cambridge: Cambridge University Press, 1995), 5–8. Table 5–1 is based on a similar table in Emans.

12. Table 5–2 is based on a similar table in Kelly, "Johann Sebastian Bach's 'Eighteen' Chorales," 2. According to Nicholas Thistlethwaite, *The Making of the Victorian Organ* (Cambridge: Cambridge University Press, 1990), 169–72, the Great Eighteen setting of "Schmücke dich" is contained in a British publication from 1838. Thistlethwaite, though, is confusing this work with another organ arrangement of this chorale listed as BWV 759, now known to be by G. A. Homilius.

13. See Hans T. David and Arthur Mendel, *The New Bach Reader: A Life of Johann Sebastian Bach in Letters and Documents*, revised and enlarged by Christoph Wolff (New York: Norton, 1998), 361. Quite ironically, Pierre Boulez's encounter with this work about two hundred years later resulted in his demand for "an alliance between material and invention"; see Jean-Jacques Nattiez, ed., *Orientations: Collected Writings by Pierre Boulez* (Cambridge, Mass.: Harvard University Press, 1986), 25.

14. See NBA IV/2, KB, 17. Mendelssohn's edition also includes the double-pedal arrangement of "Wir glauben all an einen Gott, Vater," BWV 740, a work presumably by J. L. Krebs.

15. See Robert Schumann, *Tagebücher*, edited by Georg Eismann and Gerd Nauhaus, 3 vols. (Leipzig: VEB Deutscher Verlag für Musik, 1971–87), 2:34, 40–41, 53, 55.

16. See Arnfried Edler, *Robert Schumann und seine Zeit* (Laaber: Laaber-Verlag, 1982), 292. On the same page of this study, Edler notes that Schumann also instructed his piano pupils to transcribe organ chorales by Bach.

17. "Bach's Choralbuch nach u. nach durchgespielt" (diary entry of mid-March 1837); see Schumann, *Tagebücher*, 2:34.

18. "Das nachstehende Vorspiel von J. S. Bach 'Schmücke dich, o liebe Seele' gehört zu den innigsten und lieblichsten Dichtungen dieses unerreich-

baren Meisters. Wie schön geschmückt, und doch wie rein von allem Tand geht die Hauptstimme einher!"

19. "Ich fand abends einer Wundervolle Orgel, wo ich *Schmücke dich o liebe Seele* spielen konnte nach Herzenslust." The entire letter is printed in Felix Mendelssohn-Bartholdy, *Briefe aus den Jahren 1830 bis 1847,* edited by Paul Mendelssohn-Bartholdy and Carl Mendelssohn-Bartholdy, 4th ed., 2 vols. (Leipzig: Hermann Mendelssohn, 1862–63), 1:268–71.

20. Letter of October 6, 1831. Translation adapted from Felix Mendelssohn-Bartholdy, *Letters from Italy and Switzerland,* translated by Grace (Lady) Wallace, 7th ed. (London: Longmans, Green, Reader, & Dyer, 1876), 289–90. For the original German, see Mendelssohn-Bartholdy, *Briefe,* 1:277–78. Mendelssohn is referring here to the organ at St. Peter's Church in Munich, built by Joachim Wagner.

21. "Heut hab ich den ganzen Morgen gespielt, und angefangen zu studieren, weil es eigentlich eine Schande ist, dass ich die Hauptsachen von Seb. Bach nicht spielen kann." Cited in Susanna Grossmann-Vendrey, *Felix Mendelssohn Bartholdy und die Musik der Vergangenheit* (Regensburg: Gustav Bosse Verlag, 1969), 182.

22. See Andreas Sieling, "'Selbst den alten Sebastian suchte man nicht mehr so langstielig abzuhaspeln': Zur Rezeptionsgeschichte der Orgelwerke Bachs," in *Bach und die Nachwelt,* vol. 2: *1850–1900,* edited by Michael Heinemann and Hans-Joachim Hinrichsen (Laaber: Laaber-Verlag, 1999), 300–313.

23. See Sieling, "Zur Rezeptionsgeschichte," 307.

24. Translation based on Henry Pleasants, ed., *The Musical World of Robert Schumann: A Selection from His Own Writings* (London: Gollancz, 1965), 93. For the original German, see Robert Schumann, *Gesammelte Schriften über Musik und Musiker,* 4 vols. (Leipzig: Georg Wigand, 1854), 1:219.

25. Translation from David and Mendel, *The New Bach Reader,* 502.

26. See Bodo Bischoff, "Das Bach-Bild Robert Schumanns," in *Bach und die Nachwelt,* vol. 1: *1750–1850,* edited by Michael Heinemann and Hans-Joachim Hinrichsen (Laaber: Laaber-Verlag, 1997), 499, n. 327.

27. See Carl Wehmer, ed., *Ein tief gegründet Herz: Der Briefwechsel Felix Mendelssohn-Bartholdys mit Johann Gustav Droysen* (Heidelberg: Lambert Schneider, 1959), 103–7.

28. "Musik gäbe Dir eine Freude, und Du könntest Dir von Deinem dortigen Musiker 'Schmücke Dich, liebe Seele' von Sebastian Bach vorspielen lassen!"

29. "Du sagst mir, Bachs 'Schmücke dich, o liebe Seele' möchtest Du mir vorspielen. Als ich im vorigen Jahre in Berlin war, hatte Fanny mich zur Musik eingeladen. 'Des Herren Zeit ist die beste Zeit' wurde gesungen—und ich wusste schon, was mir bevorstand! War das eine Predigt!"

30. See Marcia J. Citron, *The Letters of Fanny Hensel to Felix Mendelssohn* (Stuyvesant: Pendragon Press, 1987), 161, 164, n. 4, 176, 177, n. 16.

31. See Grossmann-Vendrey, *Felix Mendelssohn Bartholdy und die Musik der Vergangenheit*, 63; and Eric Werner, *Mendelssohn: A New Image of the Composer and His Age*, translated by Dika Newlin (London: Free Press of Glencoe, 1963), 285, 296.

32. See Rudolf Elvers, "Verzeichnis der von Felix Mendelssohn Bartholdy herausgegebenen Werke Johann Sebastian Bachs," in *Gestalt und Glaube: Festschrift für Vizepräsident Professor D. Dr. Oskar Söhngen* (Witten: Luther-Verlag; Berlin: Verlag Merseburger, 1960), 145–49.

33. Prelude No. 14 in Mendelssohn's edition, also cited by him as being incompatible with sixteen-foot pedal stops, is "Wir glauben all an einen Gott, Vater," BWV 740. In this double-pedal setting (presumably by J. L. Krebs), low pedal registers could easily obscure the thick bass texture.

34. See NBA IV/2, KB, 53.

35. See Siegmund Helms, "Johannes Brahms und Johann Sebastian Bach," *Bach-Jahrbuch* 57 (1971): 16.

36. See Johannes Brahms, *Werke für Orgel*, edited by George S. Bozarth (Munich: G. Henle, 1988).

37. See Michael Musgrave, *The Music of Brahms* (London: Routledge & Kegan Paul, 1985), 241.

38. See Reinhard Schäfertöns, "Johannes Brahms und die Musik von Johann Sebastian Bach," in *Bach und die Nachwelt*, vol. 2: *1850–1900*, edited by Michael Heinemann and Hans-Joachim Hinrichsen (Laaber: Laaber-Verlag, 1999), 220–21.

39. See, respectively, Columbia Masterworks, ML 4633; and Philips, 442 400–2.

40. "The prelude, the interludes, and the accompaniment-parts are to be kept well in the background and maintain throughout a quiet, reticent character as a contrast to the melodic part, which must be strongly accented"; see Ferruccio Busoni, *Toccata and Fugue in D Minor and the Other Bach Transcriptions for Solo Piano* (New York: Dover, 1996), 93.

41. See the preface to Johann Sebastian Bach, *Ausgewählte Choralvorspiele für Klavier übertragen von Max Reger* (*Reprint der Erstausgabe in der Titelauflage 1904*), edited by Susanne Shigihara (Stuttgart: Carus-Verlag, 1989).

42. See Orpha Ochse, *Organists and Organ Playing in Nineteenth-Century France and Belgium* (Bloomington: Indiana University Press, 1994), 155, 189.

43. At the time, Franck served as "Superintendent of Studies" at the Institute; see Karen Hastings, "New Franck Fingerings Brought to Light," *American Organist* 24, no. 12 (December 1990): 92–101.

44. See Edward Zimmerman and Lawrence Archbold, "'Why Should We Not Do the Same with Our Catholic Melodies?': Guilmant's *L'Organiste liturgiste*, Op. 65," in *French Organ Music from the Revolution to Franck and Widor*, edited by Lawrence Archbold and William J. Peterson (Rochester: University of Rochester Press, 1995), 207–9, 222–24.

45. See Sven Hiemke, *Die Bach-Rezeption Charles-Marie Widors* (Frankfurt: Peter Lang, 1994), 284, 362.

46. See Albert Schweitzer, *J. S. Bach,* translated by Ernest Newman, 2 vols. (New York: Macmillan, 1925; reprint, New York: Dover, 1966), 1:vi.

47. Stefan Hanheide, *Johann Sebastian Bach im Verständnis Albert Schweitzers* (Munich: Emil Katzbichler, 1990), 217.

48. See Michael Murray, *Marcel Dupré: The Work of a Master Organist* (Boston: Northeastern University Press, 1985), 4, 223.

49. Walter Frisch, liner notes to *Bach, Brahms: Schoenberg Orchestrations* (RCA Victor Red Seal, 09026–68658–2, 1997).

50. See Arnold Schoenberg, *Bearbeitungen I/II: Kritischer Bericht, Fragmente,* edited by Rudolf Stephan and Tadeusz Okuljar (Mainz: B. Schott's Söhne; Vienna: Universal Edition AG, 1986–88), xxv–xxviii.

51. Letter to the conductor Fritz Stiedry, July 31, 1930, printed in Josef Rufer, *The Works of Arnold Schoenberg: A Catalogue of His Compositions, Writings and Paintings,* translated by Dika Newlin (New York: Free Press of Glencoe, 1963), 94.

52. See also the discussion in Joseph N. Strauss, *Remaking the Past: Musical Modernism and the Influence of the Tonal Tradition* (Cambridge, Mass.: Harvard University Press, 1990), 45–48.

53. See James Day, *Vaughan Williams* (Oxford: Oxford University Press, 1998), 234, 312.

54. See H. L. Kirk, *Pablo Casals* (New York: Holt, Rinehart & Winston, 1974), 215–16.

55. Leopold Stokowski, *Music for All of Us* (New York: Simon & Schuster, 1943), 146.

56. A very similar orchestration of this "Nun komm" setting is that by Ottorino Respighi, which was first performed in 1930 by the New York Philharmonic. For a recording, see *Symphonic Bach: Orchestral Transcriptions by Respighi and Elgar* (Delos, DE 3098, 1991).

57. This score today forms part of the Stokowski Collection, housed at the University of Pennsylvania Libraries.

58. Recently reissued on the Pearl label; see *Stokowski: Bach Transcriptions* (GEMM CDS 9098, 1994).

59. See *Wilhelm Kempff Plays Bach* (Deutsche Grammophon, 439 672–2, 1993).

60. Hii's recording of this arrangement is included on *J. S. Bach: New Transcriptions for Guitar* (Guitar Solo Publications, GSP 1012CD, 1995).

BIBLIOGRAPHY

Apel, Willi. *The History of Keyboard Music to 1700.* Translated and revised by Hans Tischler. Bloomington: Indiana University Press, 1972. (Originally published as *Geschichte der Orgel- und Klaviermusik bis 1700.* Kassel: Bärenreiter, 1967.)

Apel, Willi, ed. *Harvard Dictionary of Music.* Cambridge, Mass.: Harvard University Press, 1944.

Archbold, Lawrence. "Towards a Critical Understanding of Buxtehude's Expressive Chorale Preludes." In *Church, Stage, and Studio: Music and Its Contexts in Seventeenth-Century Germany*, edited by Paul Walker, 87–106. (*Studies in Music*, 107.) Ann Arbor: UMI Research Press, 1990.

Bach, Johann Michael. *Sämtliche Orgelchoräle / The Complete Organ Chorales.* Edited by Christoph Wolff. (*Stuttgarter Bach-Ausgaben.*) Neuhausen-Stuttgart: Hänssler, 1988.

Bach, Johann Sebastian. *Die achtzehn grossen Orgelchoräle BWV 651–668 und Canonische Veränderungen über "Vom Himmel hoch" BWV 769. (Meisterwerke der Musik im Faksimile, 5.)* Facsimile edition of the autograph manuscript, with a preface by Peter Wollny. Laaber: Laaber-Verlag, 1999.

———. *An Wasserflüssen Babylon: Chorale Prelude by J. S. Bach, Transcribed for Orchestra by M. Wood-Hill.* London: Goodwin & Tabb, 1926.

———. *Ausgewählte Choralvorspiele für Klavier übertragen von Max Reger (Reprint der Erstausgabe in der Titelauflage 1904.)* Edited by Susanne Shigihara. Stuttgart: Carus-Verlag, 1989.

———. *Bach-Album: Sammlung berühmter Orgelcompositionen von Johann Sebastian Bach.* Edited by Ernst H. Wolfram. Leipzig: C. F. Peters, 1885.

Bach-Dokumente 1: Schriftstücke von der Hand Johann Sebastian Bachs. Edited by Werner Neumann and Hans-Joachim Schulze. Kassel: Bärenreiter; Leipzig: VEB Deutscher Verlag für Musik, 1963.

Bach-Dokumente 2: Fremdschriftliche und gedruckte Dokumente zur Lebens-geschichte Johann Sebastian Bachs 1685–1750. Edited by Werner Neu-mann and Hans-Joachim Schulze. Kassel: Bärenreiter; Leipzig: VEB Deutscher Verlag für Musik, 1969.

Bach-Dokumente 3: Dokumente zum Nachwirken Johann Sebastian Bachs. Edited by Hans-Joachim Schulze. Kassel: Bärenreiter; Leipzig: VEB Deutscher Verlag für Musik, 1972.

————. *Chorale Preludes Translated by M. Wood-Hill for String Quartet or String Orchestra.* Boston: R. D. Row, 1935.

————. *Choral: Vor deinen Thron tret ich hiermit (Wenn wir in höchsten Nöten sein), für den praktischen Gebrauch eingerichtet von Felix Oberborbeck.* Wolfenbüttel: Möseler Verlag, 1950.

————. *Choralvorspiele.* Edited by Ernst Naumann. (*Johann Sebastian Bach's Werke für Orgel: Gesamtausgabe für den praktischen Gebrauch, 8–9.*) Leipzig: Breitkopf & Härtel, 1899–1902.

————. *Choralvorspiele für die Orgel: Für das Clavier übertragen von Carl Tausig.* Berlin: Adolph Fürstner, n.d.

————. *Choralvorspiele von Joh. Seb. Bach, instrumentiert von Arnold Schön-berg.* Vienna: Universal Edition, 1925.

————. *Eighteen Large Chorales for the Organ by Johann Sebastian Bach.* Edited by Albert Riemenschneider. Bryn Mawr: Oliver Ditson, 1952.

————. *Fantasia super Komm Heiliger Geist.* Facsimile edition of the auto-graph manuscript, with a preface by Peter Wackernagel. Leipzig: Edition Merseburger, 1950.

————. *15 Grand Preludes on Corales.* Edited by Felix Mendelssohn. (*John Sebastian Bach's Organ Compositions on Corales, 3–4.*) London: Coventry & Hollier, 1846.

————. *15 Grosse Choral-Vorspiele für die Orgel von Johann Sebastian Bach.* Edited by Felix Mendelssohn. Leipzig: Breitkopf & Härtel, 1846.

————. *The Great Choral-Preludes.* Edited by William Thomas Best, revised by Arthur Eaglefield Hull. (*Johann Sebastian Bach's Organ Works, 11–14.*) London: Augener, 1914.

————. *Grössere und kunstreichere Choralvorspiele.* Edited by Friedrich Con-rad Griepenkerl and Ferdinand Roitzsch. (*Johann Sebastian Bach's Kom-positionen für die Orgel, 6–7.*) Leipzig: C. F. Peters, 1847.

————. *I. Orgelbüchlein, II. Sechs Choräle, III. Achtzehn Choräle.* Edited by Wilhelm Rust. (*Joh. Seb. Bach's Orgelwerke, 2 = vol. 25/2 of Johann Se-bastian Bach's Werke* [Bachgesellschaft edition].) Leipzig: Breitkopf & Härtel, 1878.

————. *Nun Komm' der Heiden Heiland, BWV 659.* Transcribed for solo gui-tar by Philip Hii. San Francisco: Guitar Solo Publications, 1996.

————. *Organ Choral Preludes Arranged for Pianoforte by William Murdoch.* 4 volumes. London: Schott, 1928.

————. *Organ Choral Preludes Arranged for Strings by Harry Hodge.* 2 volumes. Glasgow: Paterson's Publications, 1926.

————. *The Organ Works of John Sebastian Bach.* 3 volumes. Edited by John Pointer and John E. West. London: Novello, ca. 1895.

————. *Orgelbüchlein, 18 grosse Choralbearbeitungen, Anhang: Varianten.* Edited by Heinz Lohmann. (*Sämtliche Orgelwerke*, 7.) Wiesbaden: Breitkopf & Härtel, 1968.

————. *Die Orgelchoräle aus der Leipziger Originalhandschrift.* (*Neue Bach-Ausgabe*, series IV, vol. 2.) Edited by Hans Klotz. Kassel: Bärenreiter; Leipzig: VEB Deutscher Verlag für Musik, 1958.

————. *Orgelchoralvorspiele von Johann Sebastian Bach: Auf das Pianoforte im Kammerstyl übertragen von Ferruccio Benvenuto Busoni.* 2 volumes. Leipzig: Breitkopf & Härtel, 1898.

————. *Schübler Chorales, Eighteen Chorales, Chorale Variations.* Edited by Edouard Nies-Berger and Albert Schweitzer. (*Complete Organ Works*, 8.) New York: G. Schirmer, 1967.

————. *Thirty-five Chorale Preludes Arranged and Edited for Pianoforte by W. Gillies Whittaker.* 4 volumes. London: Oxford University Press, 1931.

————. *Twelve Chorale Preludes for Organ by Johann Sebastian Bach.* Edited by Franklin Glynn. New York: G. Schirmer, 1931.

————. *Twenty-four Choral Preludes Compiled and Arranged for Piano Solo by Felix Guenther.* New York: Edward B. Marks, 1942.

Badura-Skoda, Paul. *Interpreting Bach at the Keyboard.* Translated by Alfred Clayton. Oxford: Clarendon Press, 1993. (Originally published as *Bach-Interpretation: Die Klavierwerke Johann Sebastian Bachs.* Laaber: Laaber-Verlag, 1990.)

Basso, Alberto. *Frau Musika: La vita e le opere di J. S. Bach.* 2 volumes. Turin: Edizioni di Torino, 1979–83.

Bates, William. "An Index to the Organ Works of J. S. Bach." *Diapason* 76, no. 6 (June 1985): 9–13.

Beisswenger, Kirsten. "An Early Version of the First Movement of the *Italian Concerto* BWV 971 from the Scholz Collection?" In *Bach Studies 2*, edited by Daniel R. Melamed, 1–19. Cambridge: Cambridge University Press, 1995.

————. "Zur Chronologie der Notenhandschriften Johann Gottfried Walthers." In *Acht kleine Präludien und Studien über BACH: Georg von Dadelsen zum 70. Geburtstag am 17. November 1988*, edited by the Johann-Sebastian-Bach-Institut, Göttingen, 11–39. Wiesbaden: Breitkopf & Härtel, 1992.

Bettmann, Otto L. *Johann Sebastian Bach As His World Knew Him.* New York: Birch Lane, 1995.

Bighley, Mark S. *The Lutheran Chorales in the Organ Works of J. S. Bach.* St. Louis: Concordia, 1986.

Bischoff, Bodo. "Das Bach-Bild Robert Schumanns." In *Bach und die Nachwelt*, vol. 1: *1750–1850*, edited by Michael Heinemann and Hans-Joachim Hinrichsen, 421–99. Laaber: Laaber-Verlag, 1997.

Böhm, Georg. *Choralarbeiten und Anhang.* Edited by Johannes and Gesa Wolgast. (*Klavier- und Orgelwerke*, 2.) Wiesbaden: Breitkopf & Härtel, 1952.

Bondanella, Peter. *Italian Cinema: From Neorealism to the Present.* New York: Continuum, 1983.

Bonnet, Joseph, ed. *Historical Organ-Recitals.* 6 volumes. New York: G. Schirmer, 1917–40.

Bötel, Friedhold. *Mendelssohns Bachrezeption und ihre Konsequenzen dargestellt an den Präludien und Fugen für Orgel op. 37. (Beiträge zur Musikforschung,* 14.) Munich: Emil Katzbichler, 1984.

Bowman, David H. Liner notes to *Symphonic Bach: Orchestral Transcriptions by Respighi and Elgar.* Delos, DE 3098 (1991).

Boyd, Malcolm. *Bach. (The Master Musicians.)* Revised edition. New York: Schirmer, 1997.

———— , ed. *J. S. Bach. (Oxford Composer Companions.)* Oxford: Oxford University Press, 1999.

Brahms, Johannes. *Werke für Orgel.* Edited by George S. Bozarth. Munich: G. Henle, 1988.

Breig, Werner. "Bachs Orgelchoral und die italienische Instrumentalmusik." In *Bach und die italienische Musik,* edited by Wolfgang Osthoff and Reinhard Wiesend, 91–109. (*Centro Tedesco di Studi Veneziani Quaderni,* 36.) Venice: Centro Tedesco di Studi Veneziani, 1987.

————. "Die geschichtliche Stellung von Buxtehudes monodischem Orgelchoral." In *Dietrich Buxtehude und die europäische Musik seiner Zeit,* edited by Arnfried Elder and Friedhelm Krummacher, 260–74. (*Kieler Schriften zur Musikwissenschaft,* 35.) Kassel: Bärenreiter, 1990.

————. "The 'Great Eighteen' Chorales: Bach's Revisional Process and the Genesis of the Work." In *J. S. Bach as Organist: His Instruments, Music, and Performance Practices,* edited by George Stauffer and Ernest May, 102–20. Bloomington: Indiana University Press, 1986. (Originally published as "Zu Bachs Umarbeitungsverfahren in den 'Achtzehn Chorälen.' " In *Festschrift Georg von Dadelsen,* edited by Thomas Kohlhase and Volker Scherliess, 33–44. Neuhausen-Stuttgart: Hänssler, 1978.)

————. "Der norddeutsche Orgelchoral und Johann Sebastian Bach: Gattung, Typus, Werk." In *Gattung und Werk in der Musikgeschichte Norddeutschlands und Skandinaviens,* edited by Friedhelm Krummacher and Heinrich W. Schwab, 79–94. (*Kieler Schriften zur Musikwissenschaft,* 26.) Kassel: Bärenreiter, 1982.

————. "Textbezug und Werkidee in Johann Sebastian Bachs frühen Orgelchorälen." In *Musikkulturgeschichte: Festschrift für Constantin Floros zum 60. Geburtstag,* edited by Peter Petersen, 167–82. Wiesbaden: Breitkopf & Härtel, 1990.

Bruggaier, Roswitha. "Das Urbild von Johann Sebastian Bachs Choralbearbeitung 'Nun komm, der Heiden Heiland' (BWV 660)—eine Komposition mit Viola da gamba?" *Bach-Jahrbuch* 73 (1987): 165–68.

Bukofzer, Manfred F. *Music in the Baroque Era: From Monteverdi to Bach.* New York: Norton, 1947.

Busch, Hermann J. "Felix Mendelssohn Bartholdy und die Interpretationsgeschichte der Orgelmusik Bachs in Deutschland im 19. Jahrhundert." In

Johann Sebastian Bach: Beiträge zur Wirkungsgeschichte, edited by Ingrid Fuchs, 147–65. Vienna: Verband der wissenschaftlichen Gesellschaft Österreichs, 1992.

Busoni, Ferruccio. *Toccata and Fugue in D Minor and the Other Bach Transcriptions for Solo Piano.* New York: Dover, 1996.

Butler, Gregory G. *Bach's Clavier-Übung III: The Making of a Print. With a Companion Study of the Canonic Variations on "Vom Himmel Hoch," BWV 769.* Durham, N.C.: Duke University Press, 1990.

———. "Neues zur Datierung der Goldberg-Variationen." *Bach-Jahrbuch* 74 (1988): 219–23.

Buxtehude, Dietrich. *Sämtliche Orgelwerke.* Edited by Josef Hedar. 4 volumes. Copenhagen: Wilhelm Hansen, 1952.

Carr, Dale C. "Bach's Great Eighteen Chorale Preludes." *Organ Institute Quarterly* 11 (1964): 12–17.

Citron, Marcia J. *The Letters of Fanny Hensel to Felix Mendelssohn.* Stuyvesant: Pendragon Press, 1987.

Crowell, Gregory. "Gallomania, Marpurg, and Bach: Registration Possibilities for Bach's Late Organ Works." *American Organist* 30, no. 10 (October 1996): 63–68.

Dadelsen, Georg von. *Beiträge zur Chronologie der Werke Johann Sebastian Bachs.* (*Tübinger Bach-Studien*, 4/5.) Trossingen: Hohner, 1958.

———. *Bemerkungen zur Handschrift Johann Sebastian Bachs, seiner Familie und seines Kreises.* (*Tübinger Bach-Studien*, 1.) Trossingen: Hohner, 1957.

———. "Die 'Fassung letzter Hand' in der Musik." *Acta Musicologica* 33 (1961): 1–14.

Dähnert, Ulrich. "Organs Played and Tested by J. S. Bach." In *J. S. Bach as Organist: His Instruments, Music, and Performance Practices*, edited by George Stauffer and Ernest May, 3–24. Bloomington: Indiana University Press, 1986.

David, Hans T., and Arthur Mendel. *The New Bach Reader: A Life of Johann Sebastian Bach in Letters and Documents.* Revised and enlarged by Christoph Wolff. New York: Norton, 1998.

David, Werner. *Johann Sebastian Bachs Orgeln.* Berlin, 1951.

Daw, Stephen. "Copies of J. S. Bach by Walther and Krebs: A Study of the Manuscripts P 801, P 802, and P 803." *Organ Yearbook* 7 (1976): 31–58.

Day, James. *Vaughan Williams.* (*The Master Musicians.*) Oxford: Oxford University Press, 1998.

Dietrich, Fritz. *Geschichte des deutschen Orgelchorals im 17. Jahrhundert.* Kassel: Bärenreiter, 1932.

———. "J. S. Bachs Orgelchoral und seine geschichtlichen Wurzeln." *Bach-Jahrbuch* 26 (1929): 1–89.

Dreyfus, Laurence. *Bach and the Patterns of Invention.* Cambridge, Mass.: Harvard University Press, 1996.

Dürr, Alfred. "Bach's Chorale Cantatas." In *Cantors at the Crossroads: Essays on Church Music in Honor of Walter E. Buszin*, edited by Johannes Riedel, 111–20. St. Louis: Concordia, 1967.

————. "Heinrich Nicolaus Gerber als Schüler Bachs." *Bach-Jahrbuch* 64 (1978): 7–18.

————. *Johann Sebastian Bach: Seine Handschrift—Abbild seines Schaffens.* Wiesbaden: Breitkopf & Härtel, 1984.

————. *Kritischer Bericht* to *Neue Bach-Ausgabe*, series V, vol. 6.2 (*Das Wohltemperierte Klavier II; Fünf Präludien und Fughetten*). Kassel: Bären- reiter, 1996.

————. "Zur Chronologie der Handschrift Johann Christoph Altnickols und Johann Friedrich Agricolas." *Bach-Jahrbuch* 56 (1970): 44–63.

Dürr, Alfred, and Yoshitake Kobayashi. *Bach-Werke-Verzeichnis: Kleine Aus- gabe.* Wiesbaden: Breitkopf & Härtel, 1998.

Edler, Arnfried. *Robert Schumann und seine Zeit.* (*Grosse Komponisten und ihre Zeit.*) Laaber: Laaber-Verlag, 1982.

Edwards, Lynn. "The Thuringian Organ 1702–1720: '. . . ein wohlgerathenes gravitätisches Werk.'" *Organ Yearbook* 22 (1991): 119–50.

Eickhoff, Henry J. "Bach's Chorale-Ritornello Forms." *Music Review* 28 (1967): 257–76.

Elvers, Rudolf. "Verzeichnis der von Felix Mendelssohn Bartholdy heraus- gegebenen Werke Johann Sebastian Bachs." In *Gestalt und Glaube: Festschrift für Vizepräsident Professor D. Dr. Oskar Söhngen*, 145–49. Wit- ten: Luther-Verlag; Berlin: Verlag Merseburger, 1960.

Emans, Reinmar. "Choralvorspiele J. S. Bachs? Probleme der Zuschreibung und Echtheitskritik, dargestellt an einigen Beispielen aus der Sammlung C 55, Oxford, Bodleian Library." Unpublished paper.

Emans, Reinmar, and Michael Meyer-Frerichs. *Johann Sebastian Bach. Orgel- choräle zweifelhafter Echtheit: Thematischer Katalog.* Göttingen: Johann- Sebastian-Bach-Institut, 1997.

Emery, Walter. *Bach's Ornaments.* London: Novello, 1953.

Faulkner, Quentin. "Information on Organ Registration from a Student of J. S. Bach." *American Organist* 27, no. 6 (June 1993): 58–63. (Originally pub- lished in *Early Keyboard Studies Newsletter* 7, no. 1 [January 1993]: 1–10.)

————. *J. S. Bach's Keyboard Technique: A Historical Introduction.* St. Louis: Concordia, 1984.

Franklin, Don O. "Bach's Keyboard Music in the 1730s and 1740s: Organs and Harpsichords, Hildebrandt and Neidhardt." *Early Keyboard Studies Newsletter* 6, no. 1 (October 1991): 1–14.

Frisch, Walter. Liner notes to *Bach, Brahms: Schoenberg Orchestrations* (Houston Symphony Orchestra conducted by Christoph Eschenbach). RCA Victor Red Seal 09026–68658–2 (1997).

Frotscher, Gotthold, ed. *Orgelchoräle um Joh. Seb. Bach.* Frankfurt: C. F. Pe- ters, 1937.

Geiringer, Karl. *Johann Sebastian Bach: The Culmination of an Era.* New York: Oxford University Press, 1966.

Gojowy, Detlef. "Lied und Sonntag in Gesangbüchern der Bach-Zeit: Zur Frage des 'Detempore' bei Chorälen in Bachs Kantaten." *Bach-Jahrbuch* 58 (1972): 24–60.

Grace, Harvey. *The Organ Works of Bach.* (*Handbooks for Musicians.*) London: Novello, 1922.

Grossmann-Vendrey, Susanna. *Felix Mendelssohn Bartholdy und die Musik der Vergangenheit.* (*Studien zur Musikgeschichte des 19. Jahrhunderts*, 17.) Regensburg: Gustav Bosse Verlag, 1969.

Hanheide, Stefan. *Johann Sebastian Bach im Verständnis Albert Schweitzers.* (*Musikwissenschaftliche Schriften*, 25.) Munich: Emil Katzbichler, 1990.

Harmon, Thomas Fredric. *The Registration of J. S. Bach's Organ Works.* Buren: Frits Knuf, 1978.

Hase, Oskar von. *Breitkopf & Härtel: Gedenkschrift und Arbeitsbericht.* 5th edition. 3 volumes. Wiesbaden: Breitkopf & Härtel, 1968.

Hastings, Karen. "New Franck Fingerings Brought to Light." *American Organist* 24, no. 12 (December 1990): 92–101.

Helms, Siegmund. "Johannes Brahms und Johann Sebastian Bach." *Bach-Jahrbuch* 57 (1971): 13–81.

Hiemke, Sven. *Die Bach-Rezeption Charles-Marie Widors.* (*Europäische Hochschulschriften*, 36/126.) Frankfurt: Peter Lang, 1994.

Horn, Victoria. "French Influence in Bach's Organ Works." In *J. S. Bach as Organist: His Instruments, Music, and Performance Practices*, edited by George Stauffer and Ernest May, 256–73. Bloomington: Indiana University Press, 1986.

Horsley, Imogene, et al. "Improvisation." In *The New Grove Dictionary of Music and Musicians*, edited by Stanley Sadie, 9:31–56. London: Macmillan, 1980.

Hurford, Peter. *Making Music on the Organ.* New York: Oxford University Press, 1988.

Jauernig, Reinhold. "Johann Sebastian Bach in Weimar: Neue Forschungsergebnisse aus Weimarer Quellen." In *Johann Sebastian Bach in Thüringen: Festgabe zum Gedenkjahr 1950*, edited by Heinrich Besseler and Günther Kraft, 49–105. Weimar: Thüringer Volksverlag, 1950.

Jones, Richard D. P. "The Keyboard Works: Bach as Teacher and Virtuoso." In *The Cambridge Companion to Bach*, edited by John Butt, 136–53. Cambridge: Cambridge University Press, 1997.

Jung, Hans Rudolf. *Johann Sebastian Bach in Weimar 1708 bis 1717.* (*Tradition und Gegenwart: Weimarer Schriften*, 16.) Weimar: Rat der Stadt Weimar, 1985.

Karstadt, Georg. *Thematisch-systematisches Verzeichnis der musikalischen Werke von Dietrich Buxtehude (Buxtehude-Werke-Verzeichnis).* Wiesbaden: Breitkopf & Härtel, 1974.

Kast, Paul. *Die Bach-Handschriften der Berliner Staatsbibliothek.* (*Tübinger Bach-Studien*, 2/3.) Trossingen: Hohner, 1958.

Keller, Hermann. *The Organ Works of Bach: A Contribution to Their History, Form, Interpretation and Performance.* Translated by Helen Hewitt. New York: C. F. Peters, 1967. (Originally published as *Die Orgelwerke Bachs: Ein Beitrag zu ihrer Geschichte, Form, Deutung und Wiedergabe.* Leipzig: Edition Peters, 1948.)

Keller, Hermann, ed. *Achtzig Choralvorspiele deutscher Meister des 17. und 18. Jahrhunderts.* Frankfurt: C. F. Peters, 1937.

Kelly, Clark. "Johann Sebastian Bach's 'Eighteen' Chorales, BWV 651–668: Perspectives on Editions and Hymnology." D.M.A. dissertation, Eastman School of Music, 1988.

Kenney, Sylvia W. *Catalog of the Emilie and Karl Riemenschneider Memorial Bach Library.* New York: Columbia University Press, 1960.

Kilian, Dietrich. *Kritischer Bericht* to *Neue Bach-Ausgabe,* series IV, vols. 5 and 6 (*Präludien, Toccaten, Fantasien und Fugen für Orgel*). Kassel: Bärenreiter; Leipzig: VEB Deutscher Verlag für Musik, 1978–79.

————. *Kritischer Bericht* to *Neue Bach-Ausgabe,* series IV, vol. 7 (*Sechs Sonaten und verschiedene Einzelwerke*). Kassel: Bärenreiter; Leipzig: VEB Deutscher Verlag für Musik, 1988.

Kirk, H. L. *Pablo Casals.* New York: Holt, Rinehart & Winston, 1974.

Klingemann, Karl, ed. *Felix Mendelssohn-Bartholdys Briefwechsel mit Legationsrat Karl Klingemann in London.* Essen: G. D. Baedeker, 1909.

Klotz, Hans. *Kritischer Bericht* to *Neue Bach-Ausgabe,* series IV, vol. 2 (*Die Orgelchoräle aus der Leipziger Originalhandschrift*). Kassel: Bärenreiter; Leipzig: VEB Deutscher Verlag für Musik, 1957.

Kobayashi, Yoshitake. *Die Notenschrift Johann Sebastian Bachs: Dokumentation ihrer Entwicklung.* (*Neue Bach-Ausgabe,* series IX, vol. 2.) Kassel: Bärenreiter; Leipzig: VEB Deutscher Verlag für Musik, 1989.

————. "Quellenkundliche Überlegungen zur Chronologie der Weimarer Vokalwerke Bachs." In *Das Frühwerk Johann Sebastian Bachs,* edited by Karl Heller and Hans-Joachim Schulze, 290–310. Cologne: Studio, 1995.

————. "Zur Chronologie der Spätwerke Johann Sebastian Bachs: Kompositions- und Aufführungstätigkeit von 1736 bis 1750." *Bach-Jahrbuch* 74 (1988): 7–72.

————. "Zur Teilung des Bachschen Erbes." In *Acht kleine Präludien und Studien über BACH: Georg von Dadelsen zum 70. Geburtstag am 17. November 1988,* edited by the Johann-Sebastian-Bach-Institut, Göttingen, 67–75. Wiesbaden: Breitkopf & Härtel, 1992.

Kranemann, Detlev. "Johann Sebastian Bachs Krankheit und Todesursache—Versuch einer Deutung." *Bach-Jahrbuch* 76 (1990): 53–64.

Krapf, Gerhard. *Bach: Improvised Ornamentation and Keyboard Cadenzas—an Approach to Creative Performance.* Dayton: Sacred Music Press, 1983.

Krause, Peter. *Handschriften der Werke Johann Sebastian Bachs in der Musikbibliothek der Stadt Leipzig.* (*Bibliographische Veröffentlichungen der Musikbibliothek der Stadt Leipzig,* 3.) Leipzig: Musikbibliothek der Stadt Leipzig, 1964.

————. *Originalausgaben und ältere Drucke der Werke Johann Sebastian Bachs in der Musikbibliothek der Stadt Leipzig.* (*Bibliographische Veröffentlichungen der Musikbibliothek der Stadt Leipzig,* 5.) Leipzig: Musikbibliothek der Stadt Leipzig, 1970.

Krebs, Johann Ludwig. *Choralbearbeitungen.* Edited by Gerhard Weinberger. (*Sämtliche Orgelwerke,* 3.) Wiesbaden: Breitkopf & Härtel, 1986.

Kupferberg, Herbert. *Those Fabulous Philadelphians: The Life and Times of a Great Orchestra*. New York: Charles Scribner's Sons, 1969.

Leaver, Robin A. "Bach and Hymnody: The Evidence of the *Orgelbüchlein*." *Early Music* 13 (1985): 227–36.

———. Liner notes to *The Leipzig Chorales of J. S. Bach: Joan Lippincott, Organist*. Gothic Records, G 49099 (1998).

Löhlein, Heinz-Harald. *Kritischer Bericht* to *Neue Bach-Ausgabe*, series IV, vol. 1 (*Orgelbüchlein; Sechs Choräle von verschiedener Art [Schübler-Choräle]; Orgelpartiten*). Kassel: Bärenreiter; Leipzig: VEB Deutscher Verlag für Musik, 1987.

Lorenzen, Johannes. *Max Reger als Bearbeiter Bachs*. (*Schriftenreihe des Max-Reger-Instituts Bonn–Bad Godesberg*, 2.) Wiesbaden: Breitkopf & Härtel, 1982.

Luedtke, Hans. *J. S. Bachs Choralvorspiele*. Leipzig: Breitkopf & Härtel, 1919.

Marshall, Robert L. "Bach's *tempo ordinario*: A Plaine and Easie Introduction to the System." In *Critica Musica: Essays in Honor of Paul Brainard*, edited by John Knowles, 249–78. New York: Gordon & Beach, 1996.

———."Chorale Settings." In *The New Grove Dictionary of Music and Musicians*, edited by Stanley Sadie, 4:323–38. London: Macmillan, 1980.

———. *The Compositional Process of J. S. Bach: A Study of the Autograph Scores of the Vocal Works*. 2 volumes. Princeton: Princeton University Press, 1972.

———. Liner notes to *The Uncommon Bach: Johann Sebastian Bach Organ Works—Variants, Rarities, and Transcriptions* (performed by Joan Lippincott and George Ritchie). Pro Gloriae Musicae Recordings, PGM 115 (1997).

———. *Luther, Bach, and the Early Reformation Chorale*. Kessler Reformation Lecture, Emory University, 1995.

———. "Tempo and Dynamics: The Original Terminology." In Marshall, *The Music of Johann Sebastian Bach: The Sources, the Style, the Significance*, 255–69. New York: Schirmer, 1989. (Originally published as "Tempo and Dynamic Indications in the Bach Sources: A Review of the Terminology." In *Bach, Handel, Scarlatti: Tercentenary Essays*, edited by Peter Williams, 259–75. Cambridge: Cambridge University Press, 1985.)

May, Ernest. "Breitkopf's Role in the Transmission of J. S. Bach's Organ Chorales." Ph.D. dissertation, Princeton University, 1974.

———. "Connections between Breitkopf and J. S. Bach." *Bach Perspectives* 2 (*J. S. Bach, the Breitkopfs, and Eighteenth-Century Music Trade*) (1996): 11–26.

———. "J. G. Walther and the Lost Weimar Autographs of Bach's Organ Works." In *Studies in Renaissance and Baroque Music in Honor of Arthur Mendel*, edited by Robert L. Marshall, 264–82. Hackensack: Joseph Boonin; Kassel: Bärenreiter, 1974.

———. "The Types, Uses, and Historical Position of Bach's Organ Chorales." In *J. S. Bach as Organist: His Instruments, Music, and Performance Prac-

tices, edited by George Stauffer and Ernest May, 81–101. Bloomington: Indiana University Press, 1986.

Mendelssohn-Bartholdy, Felix. *Briefe aus den Jahren 1830 bis 1847.* Edited by Paul Mendelssohn-Bartholdy and Carl Mendelssohn-Bartholdy. 4th edition. 2 volumes. Leipzig: Hermann Mendelssohn, 1862–63.

———. *Letters from Italy and Switzerland.* Translated by Grace (Lady) Wallace. 7th edition. London: Longmans, Green, Reader, & Dyer, 1876.

Meyer, Ulrich. "Zur Frage der inneren Einheit von Bachs Siebzehn Chorälen (BWV 651–667)." *Bach-Jahrbuch* 58 (1972): 61–75.

Müller-Buscher, Henning. *Georg Böhms Choralbearbeitungen für Tasteninstrumente.* Laaber: Laaber-Verlag, 1979.

Murray, Michael. *Albert Schweitzer, Musician.* Aldershot: Scolar Press, 1994.

———. *French Masters of the Organ: Saint-Saëns, Franck, Widor, Vierne, Dupré, Langlais, Messiaen.* New Haven: Yale University Press, 1998.

———. *Marcel Dupré: The Work of a Master Organist.* Boston: Northeastern University Press, 1985.

Musgrave, Michael. *The Music of Brahms.* (*Companions to the Great Composers.*) London: Routledge & Kegan Paul, 1985.

Nattiez, Jean-Jacques, ed. *Orientations: Collected Writings by Pierre Boulez.* Translated by Martin Cooper. Cambridge, Mass.: Harvard University Press, 1986.

Near, John R. "Charles-Marie Widor: The Organ Works and Saint-Sulpice." *American Organist* 27, no. 2 (February 1993): 46–59.

Ochse, Orpha. *Organists and Organ Playing in Nineteenth-Century France and Belgium.* Bloomington: Indiana University Press, 1994.

Owen, Barbara. *E. Power Biggs: Concert Organist.* Bloomington: Indiana University Press, 1987.

———. *The Registration of Baroque Organ Music.* Bloomington: Indiana University Press, 1997.

Pachelbel, Johann. *Ausgewählte Orgelwerke.* Edited by Karl Matthaei. 4 volumes. Kassel: Bärenreiter, 1936.

Pape, Matthias. *Mendelssohns Leipziger Orgelkonzert 1840: Ein Beitrag zur Bach-Pflege im 19. Jahrhundert.* Wiesbaden: Breitkopf & Härtel, 1988.

Pfatteicher, Carl F., and Archibald T. Davison, eds. *The Church Organist's Golden Treasury.* 3 volumes. Bryn Mawr: Oliver Ditson, 1949–51.

Pirro, André. *Johann Sebastian Bach: The Organist and His Works for the Organ.* Translated by Wallace Goodrich. New York: G. Schirmer, 1902. (Originally published as *L'orgue de Jean-Sébastien Bach.* Paris: Fischbacher, 1895.)

Plantinga, Leon. *Schumann as Critic.* (*Yale Studies in the History of Music*, 4.) New Haven: Yale University Press, 1967. Reprint, New York: Da Capo Press, 1976.

Pleasants, Henry, ed. *The Musical World of Robert Schumann: A Selection from His Own Writings.* London: Gollancz, 1965. Reprint (as *Schumann on Music: A Selection from the Writings*), New York: Dover, 1988.

Polko, Elise. *Reminiscences of Felix Mendelssohn-Bartholdy.* Translated by Grace (Lady) Wallace. New York: Leypoldt & Holt, 1869.

Randel, Don Michael, ed. *The New Harvard Dictionary of Music.* Cambridge, Mass.: Harvard University Press, 1986.

Reinken, Johann Adam. *Sämtliche Orgelwerke.* Edited by Klaus Beckmann. Wiesbaden: Breitkopf & Härtel, 1974.

Richter, Klaus Peter. *Orgelchoral und Ensemblesatz bei J. S. Bach. (Münchner Veröffentlichungen zur Musikgeschichte,* 37.) Tutzing: Hans Schneider, 1982.

Ritchie, George, and George Stauffer. *Organ Technique: Modern and Early.* Englewood Cliffs: Prentice-Hall, 1992.

Ritter, August Gottfried. *Kunst des Orgelspiels.* Erfurt, 1844.

Rufer, Josef. *The Works of Arnold Schoenberg: A Catalogue of His Compositions, Writings and Paintings.* Translated by Dika Newlin. New York: Free Press of Glencoe, 1963. (Originally published as *Das Werk Arnold Schoenbergs.* Kassel: Bärenreiter, 1959.)

Schäfertöns, Reinhard. "Johannes Brahms und die Musik von Johann Sebastian Bach." In *Bach und die Nachwelt,* vol. 2: *1850–1900.* Edited by Michael Heinemann and Hans-Joachim Hinrichsen, 201–24. Laaber: Laaber-Verlag, 1999.

Schmieder, Wolfgang. *Thematisch-systematisches Verzeichnis der musikalischen Werke Johann Sebastian Bachs (Bach-Werke-Verzeichnis).* Revised edition. Wiesbaden: Breitkopf & Härtel, 1990.

Schoenberg, Arnold. *Bearbeitungen I/II.* Edited by Rudolf Stephan and Tadeusz Okuljar. (*Arnold Schönberg: Sämtliche Werke,* series B, vols. 25/26.) Mainz: B. Schott's Söhne; Vienna: Universal Edition AG, 1986–88.

Schrammek, Winfried. "Orgel, Positiv, Clavicymbel und Glocken der Schlosskirche zu Weimar 1658 bis 1774." In *Bericht über die Wissenschaftliche Konferenz zum V. Internationalen Bachfest der DDR in Verbindung mit dem 60. Bachfest der Neuen Bachgesellschaft,* edited by Winfried Hoffmann and Armin Schneiderheinze, 99–111. Leipzig: VEB Deutscher Verlag für Musik, 1988.

Schulenberg, David. *The Keyboard Music of J. S. Bach.* New York: Schirmer, 1992.

Schulze, Hans-Joachim. "J. S. Bach's Concerto-Arrangements for Organ— Studies or Commissioned Works?" *Organ Yearbook* 3 (1972): 4–13.

———. *Studien zur Bach-Überlieferung im 18. Jahrhundert.* (*Musikwissenschaftliche Studienbibliothek Peters.*) Leipzig: Edition Peters, 1984.

Schumann, Robert. *Gesammelte Schriften über Musik und Musiker.* 4 volumes. Leipzig: Georg Wigand, 1854.

———. *Tagebücher.* Edited by Georg Eismann and Gerd Nauhaus. 3 volumes. Leipzig: VEB Deutscher Verlag für Musik, 1971–87.

Schweitzer, Albert. *J. S. Bach.* Translated by Ernest Newman. 2 volumes. New York: Macmillan, 1925. Reprint, New York: Dover, 1966. (Originally published as *Jean-Sébastian Bach, le musicien-poète.* Leipzig: Breitkopf & Härtel, 1905.)

Sieling, Andreas. *August Wilhelm Bach (1796–1869): Kirchenmusik und Seminarmusiklehrer-Ausbildung in Preussen im zweiten Drittel des 19. Jahrhunderts.* (*Berliner Musik Studien*, 7.) Cologne: Studio, 1995.

————. "'Selbst den alten Vater Sebastian suchte man nicht mehr so langstielig abzuhaspeln': Zur Rezeptionsgeschichte der Orgelwerke Bachs." In *Bach und die Nachwelt*, vol. 2: *1850–1900*, edited by Michael Heinemann and Hans-Joachim Hinrichsen, 299–339. Laaber: Laaber-Verlag, 1999.

Sitsky, Larry. *Busoni and the Piano: The Works, the Writings, and the Recordings.* (*Contributions to the Study of Music and Dance*, 7.) New York: Greenwood Press, 1986.

Smith, William Ander. *The Mystery of Leopold Stokowski.* Cranbury, N.J.: Associated University Presses, 1990.

Spies, Claudio. "The Organ Supplanted: A Case for Differentiations." *Perspectives of New Music* 11 (Spring–Summer 1973): 24–55.

Spitta, Philipp. *Johann Sebastian Bach: His Work and Influence on the Music of Germany, 1685–1750.* Translated by Clara Bell and J. A. Fuller-Maitland. 3 volumes. London: Novello, 1889. Reprint, New York: Dover, 1952. (Originally published as *Johann Sebastian Bach.* 2 volumes. Leipzig: Breitkopf & Härtel, 1873–80.)

Stauffer, George B. "Bach as Reviser of His Own Keyboard Works." *Early Music* 13 (1985): 185–98.

————. "Bach's Organ Registration Reconsidered." In *J. S. Bach as Organist: His Instruments, Music, and Performance Practices*, edited by George Stauffer and Ernest May, 193–211. Bloomington: Indiana University Press, 1986. (Originally published as "Über Bachs Orgelregistrierpraxis." *Bach-Jahrbuch* [1981]: 91–105.)

————. "Boyvin, Grigny, D'Anglebert, and Bach's Assimilation of French Classical Organ Music." *Early Music* 21 (1993): 83–96.

————. "J. S. Bach as Organ Pedagogue." In *The Organist as Scholar: Essays in Memory of Russell Saunders*, edited by Kerala J. Snyder, 25–44. Stuyvesant: Pendragon Press, 1994.

————. *The Organ Preludes of Johann Sebastian Bach.* (*Studies in Musicology*, 27.) Ann Arbor: UMI Research Press, 1980.

Stiller, Günther. *Johann Sebastian Bach and Liturgical Life in Leipzig.* Translated by Herbert J. A. Bouman, Daniel F. Poellot, and Hilton C. Oswald. Edited by Robin A. Leaver. St. Louis: Concordia, 1984. (Originally published as *Johann Sebastian Bach und das Leipziger gottesdienstliche Leben seiner Zeit.* Berlin: Evangelische Verlagsanstalt, 1970.)

Stinson, Russell. *The Bach Manuscripts of Johann Peter Kellner and His Circle: A Case Study in Reception History.* (*Sources of Music and Their Interpretation: Duke Studies in Music.*) Durham, N.C.: Duke University Press, 1989.

————. *Bach: The Orgelbüchlein.* (*Monuments of Western Music.*) New York: Schirmer, 1996. Reprint, New York: Oxford University Press, 1999.

————. "The Compositional History of Bach's *Orgelbüchlein* Reconsidered." *Bach Perspectives* 1 (1995): 43–78.

————. "Some Thoughts on Bach's Neumeister Chorales." *Journal of Musicology* 11 (1993): 455–77.

Stokowski, Leopold. *Music for All of Us.* New York: Simon & Schuster, 1943.

Straube, Karl, ed. *Choralvorspiele alter Meister.* Leipzig: C. F. Peters, 1907.

Strauss, Joseph N. *Remaking the Past: Musical Modernism and the Influence of the Tonal Tradition.* Cambridge, Mass.: Harvard University Press, 1990.

Taylor, Stainton de B. *The Chorale Preludes of J. S. Bach.* London: Oxford University Press, 1942.

Terry, Charles Sanford. *Bach: A Biography.* Revised edition. London: Oxford University Press, 1933.

Thistlethwaite, Nicholas. *The Making of the Victorian Organ. (Cambridge Musical Texts and Monographs.)* Cambridge: Cambridge University Press, 1990.

Tusler, Robert L. *The Style of J. S. Bach's Chorale Preludes. (University of California Publications in Music,* 1.) Berkeley and Los Angeles: University of California Press, 1956.

Velten, Klaus. *Schönbergs Instrumentationen Bachscher und Brahmsscher Werke als Dokumente seines Traditionsverständnisses. (Kölner Beiträge zur Musikforschung,* 85.) Regensburg: Gustav Bosse, 1976.

Walther, Johann Gottfried. *Ausgewählte Orgelwerke.* Edited by Heinz Lohmann. 3 volumes. Wiesbaden: Breitkopf & Härtel, 1966.

Wehmer, Carl, ed. *Ein tief gegründet Herz: Der Briefwechsel Felix Mendelssohn-Bartholdys mit Johann Gustav Droysen.* Heidelberg: Lambert Schneider, 1959.

Weiss, Wisso, and Yoshitake Kobayashi. *Katalog der Wasserzeichen in Bachs Originalhandschriften. (Neue Bach-Ausgabe,* series IX, vol. 1.) 2 volumes. Kassel: Bärenreiter; Leipzig, Deutscher Verlag für Musik, 1985.

Welch, James. "Mendelssohn's Commemorative Bach Recital of 1840." *American Organist* 27, no. 9 (September 1993): 62–65.

Werner, Eric. *Mendelssohn: A New Image of the Composer and His Age.* Translated by Dika Newlin. London: Free Press of Glencoe, 1963.

Williams, Peter. *Bach Organ Music. (BBC Music Guides.)* London: British Broadcasting Corporation, 1972.

————. *The European Organ 1450–1850.* London: Batsford, 1966.

————. *The Organ Music of J. S. Bach. (Cambridge Studies in Music.)* 3 volumes. Cambridge: Cambridge University Press, 1980–84.

————. *Playing the Organ Works of Bach: Some Case Studies.* New York: American Guild of Organists, 1987.

Wolff, Christoph. "Bach and Johann Adam Reinken: A Context for the Early Works." In Wolff, *Bach: Essays on His Life and Music,* 56–71. Cambridge, Mass.: Harvard University Press, 1991. (Originally published as "Johann Adam Reinken und Johann Sebastian Bach: Zum Kontext des Bachschen Frühwerkes." *Bach-Jahrbuch* 71 [1985]: 99–118.)

————. "Bach and the Tradition of the Palestrina Style." In Wolff, *Bach: Essays on His Life and Music*, 84–104. Cambridge, Mass.: Harvard University Press, 1991.

————. "Chronology and Style in the Early Works: A Background for the Orgel-Büchlein." In Wolff, *Bach: Essays on His Life and Music*, 297–305. Cambridge, Mass.: Harvard University Press, 1991. (Originally published as "Zur Problematik der Chronologie und Stilentwicklung des Bachschen Frühwerkes, inbesondere zur musikalischen Vorgeschichte des Orgel-büchleins." In *Bericht über die Wissenschaftliche Konferenz zum V. Internationalen Bachfest der DDR in Verbindung mit dem 60. Bachfest der Neuen Bachgesellschaft*, edited by Winfried Hoffmann and Armin Schneider-heinze, 449–55. Leipzig: VEB Deutscher Verlag für Musik, 1988.)

————. "The Deathbed Chorale: Exposing a Myth." In Wolff, *Bach: Essays on His Life and Music*, 282–94. Cambridge, Mass.: Harvard University Press, 1991. (Originally published as "Johann Sebastian Bachs 'Sterbe-choral': Kritische Fragen zu einem Mythos." In *Studies in Renaissance and Baroque Music in Honor of Arthur Mendel*, edited by Robert L. Marshall, 283–97. Hackensack: Joseph Boonin; Kassel: Bärenreiter, 1974.)

————. "Principles of Design and Order in Bach's Original Editions." In Wolff, *Bach: Essays on His Life and Music*, 340–58. Cambridge, Mass.: Harvard University Press, 1991. (Originally published as "Ordnungsprin-zipien in den Originaldrucken Bachscher Werke." In *Bach-Interpretatio-nen*, edited by Martin Geck, 144–67, 223–25. Göttingen: Vandenhoeck & Ruprecht, 1969.)

Wolff, Christoph, ed. *The Neumeister Collection of Chorale Preludes from the Bach Circle*. Facsimile edition. New Haven: Yale University Press, 1986.

Wolff, Christoph, et al. *The New Grove Bach Family*. New York: Norton, 1983.

Wollny, Peter. "Zur Überlieferung der Instrumentalwerke Johann Sebastian Bachs: Der Quellenbesitz Carl Philipp Emanuel Bachs." *Bach-Jahrbuch* 82 (1996): 7–21.

Zehnder, Jean-Claude. "Georg Böhm und Johann Sebastian Bach: Zur Chronologie der Bachschen Stilentwicklung." *Bach-Jahrbuch* 74 (1988): 73–110.

————. "Giuseppe Torelli und Johann Sebastian Bach: Zu Bachs Weimarer Konzertform." *Bach-Jahrbuch* 77 (1991): 33–95.

————. "Die Weimarer Orgelmusik Johann Sebastian Bachs im Spiegel seiner Kantaten." *Musik und Gottesdienst* 41 (1987): 149–62.

————. "Zu Bachs Stilentwicklung in der Mühlhäuser und Weimarer Zeit." In *Das Frühwerk Johann Sebastian Bachs*, edited by Karl Heller and Hans-Joachim Schulze, 311–38. Cologne: Studio, 1995.

————. "Zum späten Weimarer Stil Johann Sebastian Bachs." In *Bachs Or-chesterwerke: Bericht über das 1. Dortmunder Bach-Symposion 1996*, edited by Martin Geck, 89–124. Witten: Klangfarben-Musikverlag, 1997.

Zietz, Hermann. *Quellenkritische Untersuchungen an den Bach-Handschriften P 801, P 802 und P 803 aus dem "Krebs'schen Nachlass" unter besonderer Berücksichtigung der Choralbearbeitungen des jungen J. S. Bach*. (Ham-

burger Beiträge zur Musikwissenschaft, 1.) Hamburg: Karl Dieter Wagner, 1969.

Zimmerman, Edward, and Lawrence Archbold. "'Why Should We Not Do the Same with Our Catholic Melodies?': Guilmant's *L'Organiste liturgiste*, Op. 65." In *French Organ Music from the Revolution to Franck and Widor*, edited by Lawrence Archbold and William J. Peterson, 201–47. Rochester: University of Rochester Press, 1995.

INDEX